A Vision of Perth

Denis Munro

Perth & Kinross Libraries

Whan I haik't up to Craigie Hill
And lookit east and west;
"In a' the world," said I to mysel',
"My ain shire is the best."

Whan I haik't up to Craigie Hill
And frae the hicht look't doun;
"There is nae place," said I to mysel',
"Mair braw nor our borough-toun."

And a' be mysel' on Craigie Hill
I spak in the Lord's ear:
"O! whan the haly bugles trill
Let me wauken up richt here."

William Soutar

ISBN 0 905452 32 x

Published by
Perth & Kinross Libraries
AK Bell Library
York Place
Perth
PH2 8EP

PERTH &
KINROSS
COUNCIL

Printed by
Cordfall Ltd
0141 572 0878

Contents

Acknowledgements

In writing this project I have drawn heavily on the work of a number of authors jotting down notes on facts, quotations and opinions which seemed relevant. I hope that in most cases I have given a full and correct attribution to the sources but I know that due to the long gap between collecting and using the information I will in some cases have used them without proper acknowledgement. My apologies where this is the case. I have made attempts to find copyright holders of photographs; again my apologies for any omissions.

I have received particular assistance from David Bowler of the Scottish Urban Archaeological Trust and from the staff of the AK Bell Library and Perth Museum who provided me with access to archive material and photographs.

I am also indebted to Marilyn Smith and Lynda Sime who patiently typed and amended the text more than was reasonable for me to ask.

Introduction

The contents of this publication defy description. They started life as a talk to the Town and Country Planning Association in the early 1990s when they were visiting Perth and needed someone from the Council's Planning department to fill a twenty minute gap in their programme by talking about how Perth had developed. The task fell to me and, finding there was nothing I could lift 'off the shelf', I researched enough to get me through the day and put the papers aside with the intention of doing a better job within the following few months. The months grew into years and, in fact, spanned a millennium giving the work, I like to think, something of an epic character. Seen in a more sober light, the output of about five pages of text per year is not impressive.

The lack of continuity and the fact that I tended to follow lines of enquiry which interested me, has meant that the style meandered from a talk to an essay to personal reminiscences which even in this final version I have not been able to resolve. My affection for Callar Fountain/Craigie Hill led me to the words of William Soutar and from there to his other social observations. Stories my mother used to tell me about trams in Perth, which at the time I hardly believed, took me to that line of enquiry. A boyhood spent watching trains at Friarton and helping my family at the Public Wash House in Canal Street explain the space devoted to those subjects. I also spent time fishing for eels in Perth Harbour (they must still be there since I did them no harm) and watching ships come and go from the Dundee, Perth and London Shipping Company for which my father worked at the time.

As a result, the content is less comprehensive than it should be but others will perhaps add to it in the same way that I have only brought together, and added to, the writing and observations of previous commentators. Where I have been critical, the criticism is intended to be kind since I do believe that while many wonderful things have been lost, Perth and its surroundings come close to the aspiration of a 1950s planning document that it be a place 'where men sing and birds whistle to the joy of the seasons'.

The decision to attempt something publishable was, however, prompted by a serious purpose: to encourage people to consider what our town centre actually looks like now and what it should look like in the future. The important buildings and features which have been lost over the years were removed, one by one, because they were worn out, destroyed by flood and fire or the site was acquired by random decisions to serve an immediate need and only rarely because of a plan developed in the community interest. Planned redevelopment dates largely from the second half of the twentieth century and, unfortunately, it has often been the most destructive to the historic urban form. The damage was done because in the general scheme of priorities the importance of fitting new development into a local tradition was thought about inadequately, or not at all. Worst of all, the concerns of those who cared were dismissed because they were 'airy fairy' or non-progressive.

The process of change is bound to continue and the start of a new millennium is a good time to decide whether we want to commit ourselves to new development based explicitly on modernism (and its latest derivatives) or on clearly expressed links with historic styles. It will soon become obvious to the reader that I favour the latter and have a very low opinion of modernist solutions in a historic location—which I still consider our town centre to be. The alternative view is perfectly tenable of course but in my experience it is a minority view and in this, as in most things, the majority must have its way. I will be criticised I am sure for nostalgia or, as William Soutar put it, 'weeping for beauty gone' and that may be partly true since I do remember fondly buildings and types of shop which have disappeared. But towns, unlike people, have a second chance at beauty and in our case it is far from gone.

For the title, I have drawn, rather pretentiously perhaps, from Prince Charles' book *A Vision of Britain* in which he put such a strong case against so much of modern architecture. A clear example of a king pointing out that some of his subjects had no clothes.

Denis Munro

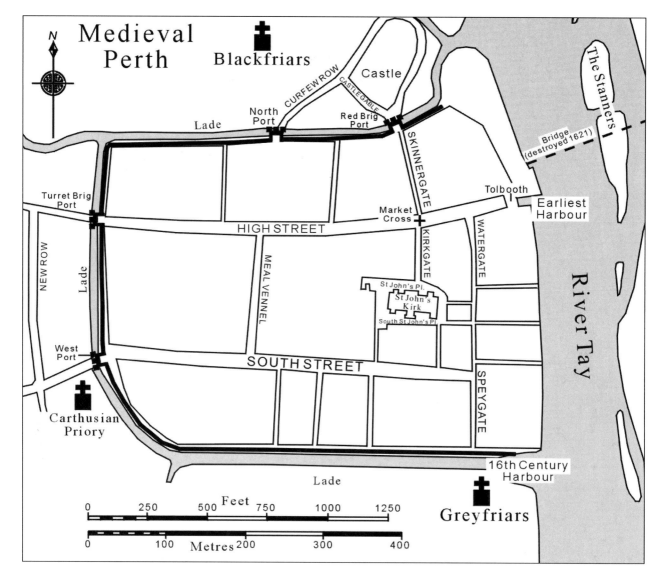

David Bowler's Map of Medieval Perth.

A Millennium or Two

many historic cities, are lost in myth and legend. As there are virtually no written records before the eleventh or twelfth century, we have to rely a great deal on supposition and informed guesswork although more and more solid information is being revealed by the work of the Scottish Urban Archaeological Trust (SUAT), who have been working steadily on the subject of 'early Perth' for some 20 years.

The romantic view is that it all started with the Romans who undoubtedly came to the area under the leadership of Agricola in AD 83. Perthshire and Angus were at the northern edge of Roman occupation in Britain and there is still clear physical evidence of Roman forts which stood as a defence against the various Scottish tribes in the Caledonian mountains to the north west. Immediately to the north of the city there is certainly a known Roman Fort at the confluence of the Almond and Tay and it has been said that the name of this camp—Bertha—was subsequently corrupted to the present place name of Perth. Those who favour a Roman explanation for the town's origins also point to the distinctive rectangular street pattern but more recent historians point out that this is also characteristic of other settlements around the Firths of Forth and Tay. There have been no archaeological finds in the city itself which point to Roman settlement and from what is known of their site requirements it is unlikely that the low, wet conditions of what is now the city centre would have appealed to them.

Town settlement probably started in the Dark Ages but the first archaeologically-verified evidence starts from the tenth century. Perth received burghal status during the reign of David I (1124–53) making it one of Scotland's earliest urban centres.

If the identity of the founding settlers is a mystery, the reasons for their choice of site can be guessed more confidently. From earliest times until the nineteenth century it lay at the highest navigable point on the Tay and the lowest bridging point. Consequently, many routes converged there. It also sits at a strategic location in fertile lowlands just to the south and east of the highland geological fault-line which traverses Scotland from south-west to north-east and the fertility of the surrounding alluvial plains must have been as valuable to early settlers as it was to subsequent farmers through each succeeding century to the present day. Even in its earliest stages of development, and certainly by the time of the first written records, it was a collecting and exchange point for agricultural produce. The Abbot of Exeter summed up the position very succinctly with a couplet from 1220:

Great Tay through Perth, through town, through country flies,
Perth the whole kingdom with her wealth supplies.

The importance of the link with the Tay is supported by recent archaeological investigations which show that the first settlement was hard against the west bank of the river—with Watergate being the earliest street—and it grew westwards pinched between the common grounds of the North and South Inches which, thankfully, local people have protected with great vigilance since medieval times. The first harbour was at the eastern end of High Street, and from its earliest days was the focus of important trade with Scandinavia, the Baltic, Low Countries and Eastern England.

If the river and the Inches have been two of the major influences on the physical form of the early burgh the third has been the Town Lade whose origins, again, can only be a matter of speculation. The Lade is a man-made watercourse which has been cut from the River Almond to the north and west of the town for a distance of some 4 miles. Such a major engineering work would hardly have been justified as a source of water supply at a time when the early settlement was beside the River Tay itself and the most likely explanation is that its justification is partly defensive and, since the eleventh century at least, as a power source for milling. Once past the City Mills, the present Lade runs under Mill Street to join the Tay at the site of a former cemetery (known as Deadlands Garden or Diddledan). In medieval times another branch, known as the Port Burn ran south by South Methven Street curving eastwards along what is now Canal Crescent and Canal Street reaching the Tay at an area known as the Coal Shore and still exists as a culvert underground. The Mill Street/Methven Street/ Canal Crescent/Canal Street lengths of the Lade certainly became an integral part of the medieval defences backed by a wall and the rectangle formed by these features appears to have contained the 'built-up area' until the end of the eighteenth century. The wall probably existed in several rudimentary forms but it is known that in 1336 a massive re-fortification took place on the instructions of Edward III who ordered that the walls were to be rebuilt with squared stones to a suitable height and with 'toweres, gates and cornices'. It is also recorded by John Harding, who visited Scotland in 1415 to spy for Henry V on the feasibility of invasion, that the ditch was 26 feet deep and 20 feet across. No visible evidence of the wall remains apart, perhaps, from a standing fragment in Albert Close but in a paper entitled 'The Sieges of Perth' a former Burgh Surveyor, Thomas McLaren, describes the wall in the following way:–

> Excavations have shown the walls to be about 8 feet thick with an inner wall of 2 feet separated from the main wall by a space of about 18 inches which was packed with clay. This lining of clay prevented the water in the ditch from percolating through the walls at high tides. The height varied according to positions from 16 feet to 18 feet. This wall would be surmounted by a thinner one forming a parapet with narrow openings called crenellations through which archers could shoot. Behind this wall was the rampart wall, a narrow path along the top of the wall sometimes protected by another parapet in the rear.
>
> . . . projecting galleries of wood were constructed first of all so that the foot of the wall could be commanded, stones being thrown through holes in the floors of the galleries. Combustible material caused them ultimately to be superseded by the projecting parapets of stone.

The first illustration of Perth, Slezer's sketch of 1693.

The Watergate. A lithographic print printed and published by Nicol of Montrose (1841). This gives some impression of what a medieval street looked like.

The Wall and the Streets Within

Apart from St John's Church all of the buildings erected prior to the mid eighteenth century have failed to survive because of the flimsy, impermanent nature of the early construction techniques or materials and the ravages of flood or fire. Although the wall too has gone, its influence and the street pattern within it have had a lasting effect on the city core.

The fortifications followed a line now defined by Canal Street, Canal Crescent, South Methven Street, Mill Street and George Inn Lane. The only streets from those times which still follow their original lines are High Street, South High Street (South Street), Watergate, Skinnergate, Speygate and Kirkgate. High Street and South Street are parallel, aligned west to east, and were both wide enough to allow vehicles to pass and to accommodate street markets. At right angles to these were less important streets like Kirkgate, Watergate, Speygate and Meal Vennel. Next in importance were the vennels whose principal purpose was to provide public access to backlands thereby making sub-division of the longer blocks possible. The last category of access was the close which was usually private allowing access for an owner to the rear of the plot.

From the West Port the road to Edinburgh followed the line of Hospital Street and Leonard Street to Craigie. The Stirling and Glasgow Road branched off this road near St Leonard's Nunnery and ran westwards past Pitheavlis Castle. The road to Crieff started from the Turret Bridge (High Street) Port with a branch at Mill Wynd through the hamlets of Balhousie and Muirton to Dunkeld and Inverness. This road was re-aligned in 1738 through the North Inch entering the town at the North Port.

All of these roads were merely paths beaten by foot and primitive vehicles along devious routes avoiding, as much as possible, watercourses and bogs. The streets within the town were roughly formed and, alternately, dusty or muddy. Refuse from the houses was deposited on them and it was normal for shop frontages to be set back 6 feet from the flats above so that pedestrians had a covered walkway. In the narrower streets this meant that the overhangs almost met in the middle. Many tenements were entered by forestairs which projected well into the carriageway.

When intensive agriculture began in the eighteenth century the need for better roads became imperative and in 1735 those leading from the two western Ports were improved. Immediately before the 1745 Rebellion the Town Council instructed the walls and the Ports of the town to be repaired and steps were taken to remove encroachments on the main streets, such as 'dyers perks, stairs, scouls and timber framing in front of low shops'.

In 1746 the Town Council instructed lamps to be erected in certain streets and appointed a person to light them. As a further improvement, the process of laying paving stones started in 1771 when squared, dressed whinstones were taken from Friarton Hill, Tayfletts and Huntingtower. After 1771 the lanes which had been behind the city walls were widened and formed into the streets now called Mill Street and Canal Street. In 1785 the Council resolved that in future all streets be paved with squared whinstones, which was the material of choice until the appearance of motor vehicles at the beginning of the twentieth century. In a brochure prepared by the Limmer and Trinidad Lake Asphalt Company summarising its work in Perth there is the comment:

In 1912–13, it was found necessary to change the method of road construction to suit changed traffic conditions and to avoid the mud and dust associated with the old order.

Atholl Street was the first to be laid with asphalt and by 1932 all of the classified roads within the burgh, extending to over 10 miles, were surfaced with this material. The Unemployment Grants Committee made arrangements for the secondary streets to benefit from similar treatment.

The general sequence in the construction of post-medieval 'new' streets and external roads was:–

1760	Edinburgh Road formed through South Inch
1769	Princes Street
1771	Bridge Lane (originally known as Queen Street).
1772	George Street
1788	Charlotte Street
1788	Act of Parliament obtained for the construction of a road from Perth to Auchterarder.
1789	New Scone Road formed.
1790–1791	Creation of a turnpike road from Crieff connected to the new bridge through Charlotte Street off which a branch was taken and named Methven Street after Lord Methven.
1793	Old Scone Road.
1801	St John Street (formed to relieve congestion of bridge traffic in Watergate)
1806	Feuing plan of lands of King James VI Hospital creating Kings Street, King James Place and south end of Scott Street.
1877	Scott Street 'extended' from Canal Street to South Street.
1893–1896	Scott Street further extended to High Street followed by Kinnoull Street from High Street to Mill Street.
1901	King Edward Street

Progress Beyond the Wall

Until the late eighteenth century the only settlement which took place outside the wall was to the west in the New Row/Mill Wynd area and to the north at the Castlegable and Curfew Row. The western suburb dates from about the fourteenth century and the northern one might have been somewhat earlier associated with the Blackfriars Monastery.

In 1766 the wall, like so many of its kind, had proved to be such a constraint on physical expansion that it was pulled down and the Lades were progressively bridged at many points to allow outward expansion. Along the southern branch of the Lade (known as the Port Burn) this bridging process was delayed by the fact that from the river to Methven Street (known as South Street Port) the waterway was broadened and made into a canal which, according to Thomas McLaren, was about 50 ft. wide and 16 ft. deep. This depth was obtained by means of sluice gates. The curve along what is now Canal Crescent was formed to allow small vessels to sail up as far as St Paul's Church where, in 1806 mooring rings were found on a part of the old city wall 10 ft. below the level of the street. For many years coal from Fife and other merchandise which came to Perth by water was brought up the canal and deposited at South Street Port which had also been the site of a fish market. As the tonnage of boats increased they could no longer reach South Street Port and therefore deposited their cargoes on the river bank at the entrance to the canal on an area which became known as the Coal Harbour. When the canal fell into disuse as a waterway permission was given to build bridges over it and it is believed that as many as a dozen bridges spanned the stretch from Canal Crescent to Tay Street.

The Coal Harbour, dating from 1539, was for a considerable time additional to, rather than a replacement for, the original one beside the High Street which remained in use into the nineteenth century. Both harbours are clearly visible on Petit's map of 1715 and Rutherford's of 1774. The move downstream was probably due to the growing size of ships, pressure on space at the end of High Street and the opportunity to transfer some cargoes to vessels capable of taking bulky goods, such as coal, along the canal developed from the Port Burn. The present harbour at Friarton dates from about 1833 and was brought fully to life in 1856 by an Act of Parliament with the stated purpose of 'enlarging, improving and maintaining the Port and Harbour of Perth; for improving the Navigation of the River Tay to the said City, and for other purposes therewith connected'.

The Act makes fascinating reading, recording far flung destinations for cargoes. Among the imports it tells us that there will be a levy of eight pennies per cwt. on elephants' teeth, tortoiseshell and nutmeg. Sporting dogs on the other hand were subject to a levy of one shilling each.

After the Tay Bridge collapse at Dundee in 1879 Perth found that its harbour trade benefited from the fact that large sailing ships which were too high-masted to pass under the bridge could now come upstream. The Town Council were therefore horrified to learn that their counterparts in Dundee were proposing that the reconstructed bridge should have a clearance of only forty feet above high water level rather than the previous eighty-eight feet. The Dundee authorities proposed this on the grounds that a lower bridge would be stronger and, from an aesthetic point of view, would be more in keeping with the beauty of their esplanade. Perth considered this an outrageous 'beggar thy neighbour' attitude and after a long-running dispute successfully petitioned Parliament against Dundee's proposals and Sir Thomas Bouch's design. Correspondence in newspapers of the day suggest that animosity between the two cities was already long established and this particular dispute was put to music by the Perth faction to the tune of 'Bonnie Dundee'.

The Tay Bridge

To the members of Council twas the Provost who spoke,
We are met to resolve, since the bridge it is broke,
That the Bridge be rebuilt, and you now must agree,
That a forty feet bridge is the Bridge for Dundee.

Come build up the Bridge, come get out a plan,
Come Bouch to the rescue, and call out your men,
For the City of Perth we don't care a flea,
And a forty feet Bridge it's the Bridge for Dundee.

Of the Esplanade's beauties preservers we are,
But the Bridge's great height its beauty did mar;
Though the Tay be shut up what matter care we,
For a forty feet Bridge is the Bridge for Dundee.

Come build up the Bridge, come get out a plan, etc

Tho' Dundee is a city, so also is Perth,
Its citizens proud of the place of their birth;
And to close up its port, they'll ne'er let it be
For a ship to be stopped by a Bridge at Dundee.

Come build up the Bridge, come get out a plan, etc

Then Perth for your river be now on your guard,
In parliament then make your voice felt and heard;
A forty feet Bridge ! ! ! why it never will be,
They'll laugh at this motion, that hails from Dundee.

Come build up the Bridge, come get out a plan:
Come Bouch to the rescue, and call out your men.
What! shut up a River, that's what we'll ne'er see,
Nor the Bridge any lower at Bonnie Dundee.

Industrialisation

Perth's medieval economy was based largely on its burghal trading privileges which were protected by law and, woollen and leather goods apart, the few industries it had were to meet only local demand. In 1556, Perth was described as having 'na industrie than that of ye craftismen yat dailie and continewalie laubor with yare boddies'. In the first half of the eighteenth century it was said that linen and salmon were the basis of Perth's economy.

To practise a trade, a citizen had to be a member of the relevant trade organisation, or incorporation, of which there were ten at the end of the seventeenth century comprising 444 freemen (men with a right to vote). The composition of their organisations in 1689 was as follows.

Guildry	157
Glovers	88
Tailors	47
Weavers	34
Wrights	34
Shoemakers	30
Bakers	22
Fleshers	16
Hammermen	14
Walkers	2

The Guildry was the most numerous Group because it included the most diverse range of occupations. Originally it consisted of dyers, surgeons, maltmen and merchants but by the later seventeenth century it also included boatmen, torch bearers, porters, carters, carriers, teachers, doctors and apothecaries.

The Hammermen were metal workers including blacksmiths, pewterers, cutters, wire drawers, nail makers and plumbers.

The Wrights consisted of masons, slaters, plasterers, glaziers and carpenters.

A fascinating analysis of the composition of these trade groups and their links with family size and wealth is contained in a thesis written by Peter Vasey (1987) which also demonstrates that many occupations were concentrated in particular parts of the burgh. Most of the metalworkers (hammermen) were located in, or near, Meal Vennel. Food and drink processing, retailing and textiles predominated in the southern half; the distributive trades in the north-east between the river and Skinnergate; leather processing just outside the northern city wall where the Town's Lade and Balhousie Lade could carry away effluent from the 'Glover's Yeards' which contained over fifty tanning pits. The retail outlets for leather goods were focused on the Skinnergate where, by 1700, the majority of glovers resided or leased booths.

In the same street, as the name suggests, some tanning also took place. During the renovation of Skinnergate House in July 2000 the Scottish Urban Archaeological Trust found a tanning pit dating from the seventeenth century at which time it would not have been, by our standards, a particularly appealing place to live. The de-hairing and removal of fat from hides involved a noxious combination of urine, lime, dog dirt (which apparently contains a de-greasing chemical) and other mysterious substances. The cleaned hides were then tanned by soaking them for a long time in an infusion of tannin, usually extracted from oak bark, which inhibits decay and, if waterproofing was required, the finished leather would be treated with oils and waxes. In both cases, the special brews

In the eighteenth century the north and South Inches were used to lay out linen for bleaching in the sunlight.

Gowrie House 1600. One of the finest buildings of the late medieval period which was under consideration for the relocation of St Andrews' University to Perth in 1697.

would be topped-up and re-used as much as possible with the residues dumped in the lade, piled on a midden heap in the backyard or poured into pits and soakaways so that, one way or another, there would be contamination of the water supply which at that time relied heavily on the use of wells.

In most medieval towns the process was carried out at or beyond the boundaries where there was an adequate water supply and where the effluents would disturb the least number of people but Skinnergate was at the heart of the medieval town so neither the trade nor the people who carried it out would be ideal neighbours.

As its defensive purpose ended, the Lade became more important to the economy of the expanding town in the eighteenth century. Water-powered mills had existed on the Lade since the eleventh century and this milling of agricultural products—corn, meal and malt—began to be accompanied by the textile industry. Linen, wool and, subsequently, cotton were processed at points along the Lade from Huntingtower through Balhousie and into the heart of the town. By 1725 there are references to 46 mills in the vicinity of Perth. Towards the end of the eighteenth century, at about the time when the wall was being pulled down, further settlement was taking place beyond its limits in the Thimblerow and Mill Wynd areas. In those days, before chemical bleaching had been perfected, the technique involved laying out cloth in sunlight and this required many flat open spaces in the surrounding countryside. The North and South Inches served this purpose and other extensive bleachfields existed beside the Lade at Tulloch, Stormontfield, Huntingtower and Luncarty.

Unfortunately for Perth, the advent of the industrial revolution in the nineteenth century meant that water-powered industries were increasingly at a disadvantage to those based on steam which gave a competitive edge to industries on or near coal fields. Perth tried to respond by specialising in particular products such as umbrella cloths, handkerchiefs, napkins and gingham but by the 1840s there was considerable hardship among weavers. An article in the Perthshire Constitutional dated 10 May 1916 describes the death of Perth's oldest weaver at the age of 90 and reports that in 1834 there were 2,000 handloom weavers in the city. The Town Council tried to help by employing them on public works in what would now be called a 'job creation' scheme. One of these was raising the banks of the Tay at the North Inch and laying out the circular walk. Fortunately, the softness and purity of the local water meant that dyeing—and subsequently cleaning—was able to compensate for the decline of textile manufacturing. By 1824 there were eight dyeworks on the Lade merging progressively until Pullar's had eclipsed them all. At the end of the nineteenth century Pullar's employed some 2,000 people.

In 1796 it was recorded that some 30,000 sheep and lamb skins were cured in the town each year as well as hides and calf skins. From these skins between 2,000 and 3,000 dozen pairs of gloves were made as well as shoes and boots.

During the second half of the eighteenth century printing and publishing grew to considerable importance from small origins. The reasons for this are not entirely clear but the existence of local raw materials from paper mills at Almondbank and leatherworks and the ability of linen printers to transfer their skills to books were probably important factors as were, perhaps, a relatively educated and affluent population. The Morison family were pre-eminent among the publishing businesses of the day recording the production of 14,000 volumes in the first six months of 1794. Other commercial activity included the export of salmon to the London market packed with ice saved from the winter. One smack would sail every four days during the fishing season and would do the journey in under a week. For the return journey the cargoes were porter, cheese and groceries.

In the sixteenth to eighteenth centuries all of the fashionable addresses for nobility and merchants were—though this is difficult to imagine today—in the Watergate where many properties had large plots with a river frontage. The 'roughest' parts were in the Thimblerow area where the weavers lived.

In the vicinity of Watergate stood the Gowrie House which came close, in 1697, to being used for a relocation of St Andrews University to Perth. At that time many scholars thought that St Andrews was too remote for a thriving university and there had, furthermore, been disputes between the burgh and the university authorities.

The university chancellor, the Earl of Tullibardine, opened negotiations with the Magistrates and Town Council of Perth and a deputation was sent to find out the cost and practicalities of finding suitable accommodation. After some prevarication on grounds of cost the Town Council offered the Gowrie House as accommodation and 20,000 merks by way of removal expenses. The university demanded more money and larger premises. By May 1698 the Council had estimated that the cost would be as much as 80,000 merks which was too high a price to pay and the scheme foundered.

If the deal has been concluded it would have saved a fine building but ruined a good joke—that God was showing his sense of humour when he gave Dundee the university and Perth the prison.

In the early eighteenth century the most affluent area had moved close to the Mercat Cross (where Kirkgate and Skinnergate meet High Street) with property values declining in all directions from there.

McFarlane's map of Perth 1792. This shows, in concept form, proposals for the layout of the former Blackfriars' lands to form Rose Terrace, Barossa Street and adjacent blocks.

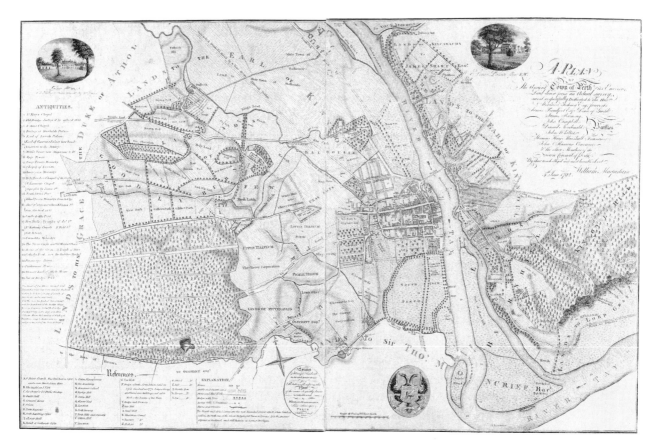

Georgian Expansion

The Georgian 'new town' expansion at Rose Terrace, Atholl Street, Atholl Crescent and its counterpart at the southern face of the city, Marshall Place, epitomises the best of our urban heritage. These streets and others such as George Street and St John Street, owe their existence to an enterprising group of families who, through their wealth and influence, controlled the government of the city from the second half of the eighteenth century until 1832 when the Reform Act gave a wider range of citizens a say on who their leaders would be.

The ruling elite, known as 'The Beautiful Order' comprised Robertsons, Sandemans, Fechneys, Stewarts, Duncans, Ramsays, Caws, Allisons and Marshalls whose names are well represented in the roll of Provosts. One of these, Thomas Marshall, is particularly bound up with urban development of this period because of his association with Marshall Place and Rose Terrace, named after his wife Rose. Marshall did, indeed, oversee most of this expansion, but the concept, land assembly and site preparation, have to be credited to his father-in-law Thomas Anderson who laid out a plan for the former Blackfriars lands extending from West Mill Street to what is now Barossa Street. The full extent of his vision can be seen on MacFarlane's map of 1792 which shows the proposed street blocks in a pattern which is immediately recognisable today.

In 1795 Anderson also laid down the conditions which would govern how Rose Terrace was to be built. Each purchaser had to build, within two years, a house of stone with ashlar front, and roof of blue slate, of the same colour as that of the three houses already erected; the houses to consist of a vault and a ground floor with two storeys and garrets above. Each householder would have 112 feet of land behind his house which was not to be used for the making of soap or candles, glass or vitriol, nor for boiling yarn, slaughtering or copper-smithing, nor for a 'Chymistry's Laboratory', nor for any other purposes which might give offence to neighbours. Each was to lay paving stones in front of his house and to make, and keep, a grass bank sloping down to the open lade which still ran between the terrace and the North Inch. To his eternal credit Anderson also laid down a condition that no further houses should be built on the north side of Charlotte Street/Atholl Street in order to keep open the extensive view over the North Inch for those streets.

By 1799 Anderson's finances were rather shaky but his daughter Rose was seen as a considerable catch with a 'tocher' of £3,000. The lucky man was Thomas Marshall a leading member of the Beautiful Order, the son of a former Treasurer, Provost, merchant and founder member of the Perth Banking Company of 1787. Thomas filled many of the positions held by his father and by 1795 had moved into property development, building what we now know as Atholl Crescent. To the city's benefit, he negotiated an exchange of land with the Earl of Kinnoull which doubled the size of the North Inch and allowed a race course to be formed on it.

Thomas and Rose lived on the first floor of one of the new houses in Charlotte Street above a shop and below a minister who kept chickens in the basement. Across the street, in lodgings, lived the Earl of Elgin (who brought to Britain the Greek artefacts known subsequently as the Elgin Marbles) and, when Thomas was away from home, Elgin and Rose were seen to exchange signals from their windows and sent each other frequent notes. Servants subsequently testified that they constantly walked about Perth arm in arm; that he visited her late at

night and they sat together in the gloaming, refused to have candles brought, and even blocked up the keyhole so that they should not be watched; and, finally, that they went up Kinnoull Hill (which was said to have a bad reputation) and disappeared into a thicket there. They had, in fact, been followed up the hill by her parents who found the climb too steep and paid the wood-keeper's nineteen year old son to complete the observation. In a belated attempt to introduce some discretion into her assignations Rose arranged for her servants to take a settee, a grate for a fire, some chairs, silver spoons and sweetmeats from Charlotte Street to the mansion which was being built for her and Thomas at the corner of Rose Terrace and Atholl Street, all of which were quickly retrieved when his return from London was announced.

A view of Perth as Dr Dibden must have seen it in 1837.

The Earl soon left Perth but she then took up with a Dr Harrison, another soldier, to whom she gave gifts of a ring and lace handkerchiefs which she had specially embroidered. In a letter she declared her affection for him and distress that he was about to leave Perth. She later admitted that she loved him better than her husband and allowed 'a feeling to develop which she ought to have repressed.' She also admitted bribing the servants to carry her letters and gifts to him and to keep quiet about what was going on.

In 1796 Thomas started divorce proceedings but not before he found out that his father-in-law was bankrupt and the £3,000 tocher did not exist. Within a matter of weeks Rose was turned out of their home and went to live with her parents until, through public ridicule, she was forced to move to Edinburgh, Yorkshire (where she again came in contact with Lord Elgin) and then to London.

By 1800 she was back in Edinburgh with her parents and enjoying the company of the armed forces again. This time she was actually seen in bed with an officer lodging in her father's house and after one of her late night visits to a Lieutenant Edgar of the Royal Artillery 'her corsets and various other articles' had to be returned to her the following morning. Provoked, no doubt, by such fun-loving behaviour Thomas renewed his divorce proceedings and, so far as one can tell, never moved to the distinguished mansion house at the corner of Rose Terrace. He died in 1808 with an obituary to be proud of:–

[it was] impossible to convey an adequate idea of the sorrow and regret universally produced in this place by the death of our late Chief Magistrate, Mr Marshall of Glenalmond. . . . His remains were brought from his late residence Bowerswell Lodge, attended by his relatives together with the Duke of Atholl. . . . The crowd which attended was immense, men, women, children pressing forward to witness the final scenes . . . every warehouse and shop was shut.

. . . it is impossible to turn the eye to any quarter of the town or its environs without some remarkable remembrance of Provost Marshall coming into view. He had a particular pleasure in planning, and a particular energy in carrying out, whatever appealed to him as calculated to adorn, improve or, in any way, be beneficial to his native town.

. . . As a private gentleman, he was no less respected and beloved— affable, courteous and pleasing in his manners; he would be a barbarian indeed who could be at enmity with him.

I am conscious that the above account of the life of Thomas Marshall strays into more detail than is necessary in a description of urban development and I defend it only on the grounds that it is more interesting. We can imagine the entertainment this saga gave to the great mass of Perth people who were not members of The Beautiful Order and perhaps it also demonstrates that, while our surroundings may change, human nature is constant.

Marshall's Legacy

Marshall's work was at the perimeter of the town until Victorian expansion took place and, although we can still appreciate it today, its original splendour was well summarised in the following account written by a Dr Dibdin in 1837 during a visit to Perth as a guest of Lord Gray.

On descending from the heights, the whole town has a fine aspect, reminding me, I know not why, of the smart, cheerful air of a provincial town in England. A broad and noble bridge of stone bestrides the River Tay. To the right is a beautiful racecourse of rich turf, enfiladed by the river, and having to the left some fine street scenery. But what most struck me, on my first approach to Perth—descending from the upper road to Kinfauns Castle—was the Water Works, of which Mr Professor Anderson had both the construction and direction. Here was a lesson to learn—or a model to copy—for all England. Here was deformity converted into beauty, and a nuisance rendered a picturesque accessory.

Despite this period of new construction there was very little outward expansion beyond the physical limits of the original walled town. Apart from the Georgian 'suburbs', much of the new development was superimposed on the medieval core either by demolishing it and putting something new in its place—George Street, St John Street and Princes Street—or in sub-division of the more spacious feus. The citizens were, in a manner which remains very familiar to planners today, making much more intensive use of available space and altering its previously loose-knit character.

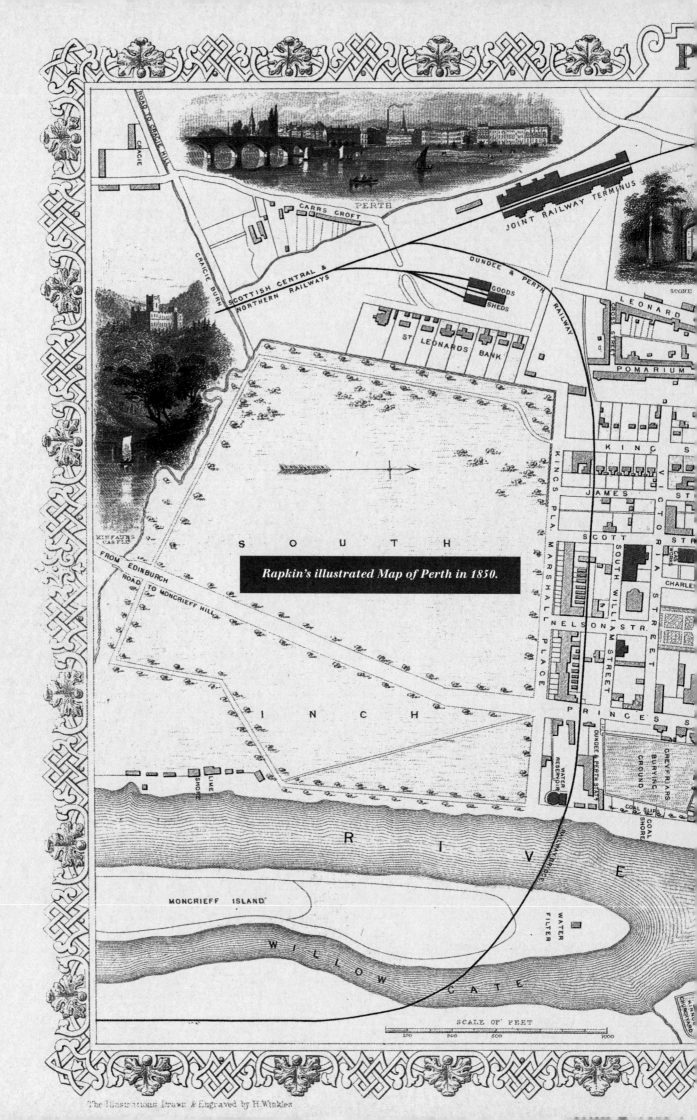

Rapkin's illustrated Map of Perth in 1850.

PERTH

P

ROAD TO CRAIGIE HILL

CRAIGIE

CARRS CROFT

JOINT RAILWAY TERMINUS

DUNDEE & PERTH RAILWAY

SCONE

SCOTTISH CENTRAL & NORTHERN RAILWAYS

CRAIGIE BURN

GOODS SHEDS

LEONARD

CROSS STREET

ST LEONARDS BANK

POMARIUM

KINFAUNS CASTLE

KING S

KINGS PLA.

VICTORIA STREET

JAMES

SCOTT

CAS WORKS

STR

SOUTH

MARSHALL PLACE

SOUTH WILLIAM STR.

CHARLES

Rapkin's illustrated Map of Perth in 1850.

FROM EDINBURGH

ROAD TO MONCRIEFF HILL

NELSON

PLACE

INCH

PRINCES

WATER RESERVOIR

DUNDEE & PERTH STAT

GREYFRIARS BURYING GROUND

LIME SHORE

COAL SHORE

R   I   V   E

RAILWAY BRIDGE

MONCRIEFF ISLAND

WATER FILTER

W   I   L   L   O   W   G   A   T   E

ST LEONARDS CHURCHYARD

SCALE OF FEET

100   300   500   7000

The Illustrations Drawn & Engraved by H. Winkles

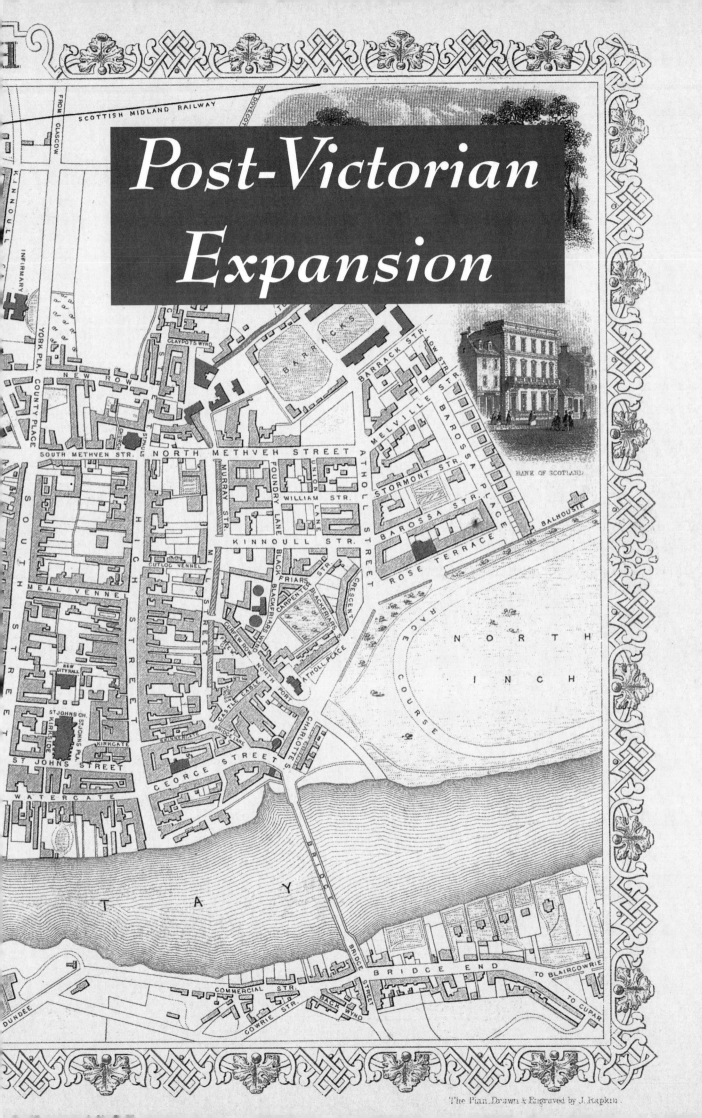

Post-Victorian Expansion

BANK OF SCOTLAND

The Plan Drawn & Engraved by J. Rapkin.

huge physical expansion which has taken place since the date of Rapkin's map of the city (1850) when the population was 22,232, it is helpful to consider developments under three important topic headings rather than following events in strictly chronological order.

Transport

The first reference to a bridge over the Tay at Perth is in 1202 and this, apparently, is also the first reference to a bridge anywhere in Scotland. Maintaining the early bridge against flood and structural failure proved to be a heavy burden on the medieval community. From 1529 onwards revenue paid to the Crown was given back in annual grants towards repairs recognising that the 'Proviest, bailies and communitie has alreadie deburssit lairge and sumpuous espense upon betting and repairing thereof'.

In 1583 five bows of the bridge collapsed into the river and the burgh began a voluntary collection for its repair but with no lasting benefit since a major part of it again collapsed in 1602. In 1621 the whole structure was swept away in a major flood. No replacement was constructed until 1772, to a design by John Smeaton, which set the carriageway high above the river so that the bridge would be flood-proof and navigable. This meant that it had to be approached by a steep ramp and could not fit in near the end of the High Street like its predecessors. The only suitable location was therefore at the north edge of the

The first rail connection to Perth was from Dundee in 1847. In the first instance the terminus was at Barnhill but within a few years the Tay had been bridged on a wood superstructure which had an opening span to allow ships to pass upstream.

Several sites, including the South Inch, were considered for the General Railway Station (there was another at Princes Street). Despite the fact that railways and the glass and iron construction techniques used over the platforms were at the leading edge of technology and innovation at that time, Victorian architects and the public saw nothing incongruous about the use of a 'Historic' style for the design of the buildings. This of course was before the advent of modernists and their phobia about 'Pastiche'.

medieval town with the result that Charlotte Street was formed to make a link with Dunkeld Road and George Street (1772), St John Street and Princes Street (1769) to connect with Edinburgh Road. The bridge itself was constructed from sandstone quarried at Quarrymill and barged down the river to the construction site.

While these operations were undoubtedly the most important early examples of the city being adapted to suit the needs of vehicles they were not the first— that distinction seems to go to the Mercat Cross which had been located in the centre of High Street at its junction with Skinnergate and Kirkgate. It was removed in 1764. Two years later the Ports were removed because they were too narrow to allow the passage of large carriages.

The construction of Smeaton's Bridge gave considerable impetus to the development of Bridgend throughout the nineteenth century and, on a national level, improved links with the north-east of Scotland.

At that time a coach journey between Edinburgh and Perth took eleven hours. Bulk cargoes could really only be moved by ship which, since the original burgh charter was granted, had been the basis of Perth's trade with the outside world.

In the second half of the seventeenth century, at a low period in Perth's economic and social fortunes, local merchants invested in a number of maritime ventures all of which were unsuccessful and did nothing to boost the burgh's wealth. The most curious of these was the construction of a ship at Rotterdam, funded by wealthy Perth merchants, and laden with cargo valued at £20,000 Scots. Her name was the Eagle of Perth and she sank at the mouth of the Tay on her maiden voyage. Two years later a second Eagle of Perth was constructed, this time at Leith, and after several voyages to Holland the master, George Fergussone 'ranne away with her . . . and never returned from Virginia againe'. On this occasion the loss was calculated to be over £10,000 Scots and, as a triumph of hope over experience, a third vessel from Rotterdam was financed by various local merchants and lost at Cockenzie at a cost of £4,000 Scots.

A new harbour was formed at Perth in 1845 and, on the Tay itself, schemes to improve navigation were undertaken. These helped to increase the size of ships which could be accommodated but the very deep draught of the early steam ships meant that Perth Harbour declined in importance during the nineteenth century. The limitations which this imposed on local commerce could have been very serious but for the arrival of the railway in the middle of the nineteenth century. The Dundee and Perth railway was opened in 1847 with a terminus, in the first instance, on the east bank of the Tay at Barnhill. When the first railway bridge was built several years later it had a swing span to allow ships to go further upstream but it was made of wood and was replaced after fourteen years. The first station on the west bank of the river was at Princes Street and the general station was opened in 1863 as the interchange between the north, west, south and east coast lines. This made the town a very important nodal point on the rail network and, in turn, led to railway-related employment being one of the principal sources of jobs for over a hundred years. The grandeur of the Station building and the sheer scale of the railway operational land which is evident on post war maps and aerial photographs, serve as reminders of an importance which is difficult to imagine today.

An interesting planning issue in its own right was the deeply divisive dispute which developed from the Town Council's willingness to allow at least one third of the South Inch to be occupied by a railway terminus. An aspect of the controversy which would be instantly familiar to anyone who follows current planning issues was the Council's fear that if they did not agree to the demands of the railway companies the terminus investment would be lost to another town. Also, the opposition, although comprising a broad alliance of citizens, was led by genteel families in Marshall Place and Leonard Bank. In terms that would do credit to any modern planning consultant they addressed the Town Council with blunt indignation:–

> The petitioners consider the North and South Inches as the pride and ornament of Perth and therefore deplore any encroachment on them which would deface their beauty.

In such circumstances it is always a good tactic to suggest alternative sites which would get the offending development away from your door and the objectors in this case were well up to the task: they suggested County Place, the Newrow and land to the south of the South Inch belonging to the Moncreiffe family. The last of these aroused the interesting fear that if the general terminus were at Friarton, commerce would follow and a rival city develop with Perth as a mere suburb. This conclusion gives some idea of the benefits expected from the arrival of the railway which did, in fact, prove crucial to the town's future growth and prosperity. It was the catalyst which brought together lowland grain with highland malt from various distilleries and enabled the distribution of the finished product to customers. Local entrepreneurs with the names of Arthur Bell, George Sandeman, John Dewar and Matthew Gloag were able to grow from being local wine merchants to companies of national and international prominence through the connections developed with London and the outside world by the railway.

Agricultural produce could be distributed to a wider market which was particularly fortuitous since yields were improving through agricultural improvements. The town's traditional role as a market for cattle and sheep became much more important when the animals could be brought and distributed by the rail network. It was no accident that Hay's and MacDonald Fraser's Marts both grew up beside the railway. Pullars which had been a bleaching and dyeing company of largely local significance, was able to grow to become a company of national and international importance in these activities, and dry cleaning, through its access to the rail network.

In the twentieth century the road network has, of course, displaced ship and rail links as the essential element of economic prosperity and it is generally acknowledged that since some 90 per cent of Scotland's population can be reached within a 90 minute drive from the city, accessibility is probably the single most important reason for new businesses locating here.

The 'accessibility' theme is currently at the heart of the Council's promotional efforts to entice investment to the city but neither the effort, nor the message, is so very different from that of an earlier Council which in 1931, reported in a *Perthshire Advertiser* article, was promoting itself to potential American industries on the following grounds:–

(a) plentiful supplies of coal and iron within easy reach
(b) material imported from the USA may be shipped direct to Glasgow and thence to Perth by rail or road
(c) the finished product may be shipped direct from Perth harbour in vessels of not more than 300 tons or despatched by rail

Perth is a very favourable place for either rail or road transport as it is situated at the junction of the principal Scottish railways, and also the principal roads between Scotland and the South.

Before the railways came to Perth the district of Craigie was open farmland, the only buildings being a few thatched cottages, but at the turn of the century the station and its associated activities made this the fastest expanding suburb of the city.

Trams

If the railways linked the citizens with the outside world, the introduction of trams as the first public transport system affected the internal daily life of the city much more directly. Only the most prosperous families had a means of personal transport and, without this, there were very practical reasons why people could not spread out from the core of the town where most of them worked and obtained their daily services. With so many transport options available to most families today it is difficult to imagine the limitations which lack of mobility imposed on people before the beginning of the twentieth century—one writer referred to it as the 'tyranny of distance'—but however ambivalent we may feel about the issue of mass transportation today, railways and trams were a liberating influence on the lives of people from the Victorian

period onwards. This had been foreseen in the slightly jaundiced view of the Duke of Wellington who deplored the railways on the grounds that 'they would encourage the working classes to move around unnecessarily'.

By the end of the nineteenth century some 30,000 people were living in a fairly tight circle of development around the medieval core and if, as we shall see, public health issues created the need for them to spread out it can equally be said that a public transport system enabled them to do so.

The first link was between Scone and Perth and appears to have arisen from a need for Scone folk to look increasingly to Perth as a source of employment when their local weaving industry declined and, at the same time, a desire by many Perth families to move out to a more healthy rural environment and thus became the first commuters. A group of local businessmen, seeing the commercial opportunities, formed 'The Scone and Perth Omnibus Company Ltd' which ran six horse buses per day in each direction from Scone to the Cross at the foot of Perth High Street or the Station entrance in Glasgow Road. On market days two further runs were made to the village of Balbeggie.

In May 1894 the omnibus company was taken over by a newly formed Perth and District Tramways Company Ltd which ran its first services, still horse drawn, on 17 September 1895 on a 3' 6" gauge track. The initial Rose Crescent/High Street/Kincarrathie/Scone link was very quickly followed by a connection to the General Station and the fact that records show this to have been carrying some 25,000 passengers per month gives an interesting insight into the extent to which local people were travelling by train. An extension to the tram route was therefore quickly made to Priory Place with the first service commencing in April 1898.

The run from Perth to Scone took twenty-five minutes behind a team of two horses supplemented by 'trace' horses in order to assist the normal team of two on the gradients at St Leonard's Bank and from George Street to Perth Bridge. These limitations, and the desire to move from something slow and safe to fast and dangerous, led to some hair raising experiments with petrol powered trams which jumped the tracks and failed in other ways requiring, in many instances, to be towed back to the Scone Depot by horses. A changeover to electric traction came in 1904 mainly, it appears, because electric street lighting was being introduced to Perth at that time and the Town Council had been obliged by Parliament to spend some £7,000 on making the new Victoria Bridge suitable for carrying electric cars. This proved to be a particularly wasteful expenditure since none of the subsequent services actually crossed the Victoria Bridge.

In the pre-electrification era the operating company had repeatedly declared a 4 per cent dividend and the interest of the Town Council had been aroused by the system. They bought the company for £21,800 and on 7 October 1903 the first services ran under the title 'Perth Corporation Tramways'. The investment in laying new tracks, electrification and extending the system to some seven track miles resulted in expenditure by the Council which in modern values would be equivalent to over £4 million. This proved to be a considerable financial burden and one which could not be serviced by matching income. The Corporation were required by statute to set aside each year a Sinking Fund to meet the capital cost of the undertaking which would have been repaid by 1935 through annual payments of some £5,000. By the end of the first year the system had run up a deficit of £3,500 (equivalent to £202,000 at 1995 values) and the Council had exhausted its borrowing powers. To break out of the financial

Opposite:
Perth's first tram service ran from Scone to Perth in the late nineteenth century. The change-over to electric traction came in 1904.

predicament various special fare options were considered including extensions to the system—the most surprising of which was a proposal to take the track to within 150 yards of the Kinnoull Hill summit, accompanied by a tearoom at the top. Sunday running was proposed, and resisted, until a limited service was introduced in April 1910. The added problems of war-time shortages and lack of investment between 1914 and 1918 meant that the system required a scale of expenditure which the Corporation was in no position to make. After the consideration of various reports it decided in February 1927 to substitute bus services for the existing tram services. An immediate trade war between the Corporation buses and those of a rival private operator very quickly put paid to the future of the trams and the last service ran in January 1929.

The only lasting physical traces of the tram system are a few lengths of track at the former depot in Scone and the rosettes on some of the High Street and George Street facades which supported the electric cables. The importance in city development terms has, however, been much more permanent, as can be seen from the map showing how, by 1928, the tram and bus routes together had both served, and led, development well towards its present perimeter. Even with hindsight, it is hard to see how the trams could ever have operated on a truly commercial basis and yet, if it had been possible to keep the system in operation to benefit from the new housing schemes which opened up after the late 1920s, there might have been some hope. These did, of course, have bus services which, from 1934, were taken over by William Alexander's company.

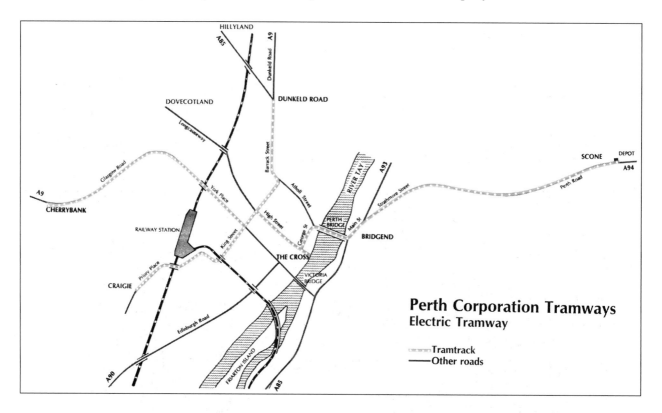

The network of tram routes by the time the service ceased in January 1929.

The Motor Car

Sir Alexander Muir Mackenzie writing in 1906 on 'Auld Perth' said nostalgically that:

> The tallow candle of our youth has been driven out by the electric light, and the hoot of the motor has supplanted the tuneful horn of the four-in-hand.

The print of Frew's Garage at Canal Street/Princes Street in 1922 shows that there was a thriving sale and repair activity in the earliest part of this century and the former Burgh Surveyor's records refer to eight car parking attendants in the early 1930s. There are also references to 'traffic congestion' in South Street and the High Street in the 1940s. Successive censuses since 1951 have shown that Perth has had one of the highest rates in Scotland of car and home ownership and these two factors have been powerful influences in promoting the outward spread of the city. During the second part of the twentieth century, owning a car allowed people the option of living in suburbs but also in villages at some distance from the traditional town centre. The owners also want to have this precious possession garaged or parked within the boundaries of their property and, when combined with aspirations for a second car, a caravan and a garden, the form of new development is much more spread out and at much lower densities than would have been imagined in any earlier period. The 1991 Census showed that 55 per cent of households in Perth had access to at least one motor car and the problems which this has created need hardly be described

By the 1930s the first 'parking attendants' were also on the scene and the Burgh Surveyor was reporting problems of traffic congestion.

to anyone familiar with the city. Until very recently it had been thought (here as elsewhere) that the challenge was to adapt the city to accommodate vehicles in ever increasing numbers and, as recently as 1972, plans had been formulated by the Burgh Surveyor's Office to create a one-way ring road system based on Caledonian Road/Atholl Street/Charlotte Street/Tay Street with a southern link forced through to the south of South William Street. Hand in hand with this, sites had been earmarked for six multi-storey car parks. Fortunately it is beginning to be accepted that we cannot continue to plan for the unrestrained use of the private vehicle—particularly by commuters—in the town centre.

The car arrives as this photo of Frew's Garage shows c.1922.

Public Health

Lewis Grassic Gibbon has a reference in one of his novels to a semi-fictional small town of Segget which the locals had summed up in the following rhyme:

Oh, Segget it's a dirty hole,
A kirk without a steeple,
A midden-heap at ilka door,
And damned uncivil people.

Unlike Segget, Perth has had a kirk with a steeple since medieval times and who can believe that it ever had 'uncivil people'. In a way that might be difficult to imagine nowadays it must, however, have had sights and odours which would make us blanch. There would, in 'pre-sanitation' times, have been cess pits in every feu and much of the human and animal excrement might have been taken away in carts both as a valued fertiliser for surrounding agricultural land and also as a source of chemicals—particularly for the local bleaching and dyeing industry. But, as the physical extent of the town did not increase much over a period of 700 years, the increasing population was largely being accommodated in the same physical space. Conditions proved ripe for a near disastrous outbreak of bubonic plague in 1349 and in later times there were recurrent epidemics which modern science would trace to poor sanitation and polluted water supply. For as long as there had been human settlement water was drawn from three sources: the Lade, draw wells and the Tay. While the Lade was being used principally as a power source for industry it would have been clean but with the advent of chemical-using processes such as bleaching and dyeing it became increasingly putrid as did the wells because of the very high water table and the fact that the water they contained had filtered through successive cess pits and middens.

To address this increasingly intolerable problem the Council asked Dr Adam Anderson, the Rector of the Academy, to come forward with a scheme for a pure supply of drinking water. After evaluation of several alternatives, he proposed a system based on piping water under the Tay from a well on Moncrieffe Island to a reservoir on top of a very fine, classically inspired, waterworks on a site at the corner of Marshall Place and Tay Street. The water was drawn into the works by a steam engine and distributed from the reservoir into pipes connecting to distribution points throughout the town. The system came into operation in 1832 and made a dramatic improvement to the quality of the supply although, disappointingly, it did not prevent an outbreak of cholera in the same year. Initially the distribution was limited to an area which could be served by gravity from the Marshall Place reservoir and that, in itself, served to limit the extent to which new development could be separated from the traditional core.

The main distribution continued to be through street wells which, by contamination and, surprisingly, vandalism, seemed partly to negate the advantages of the new, clean source. By 1860 a new reservoir was constructed at Wellshill enabling westwards expansion of the town and, on the east bank, a supply was provided by the Bridgend of Perth Water Company, drawing on local springs.

The Marshall Place facility remained in operation until 1965 when the new Water Works opened at Gowans Terrace. It feeds a network of principal reservoirs at Burghmuir, Viewlands and Muirhall.

The city's first source of pure drinking water came from the waterworks (1832) designed by Dr Adam Anderson, the Rector of Perth Academy, at the request of the Town Council. The water was drawn through gravel beds in the Tay by a steam engine, pumped to a reservoir in the dome and distributed by gravity throughout the town. Described, very aptly, by a visitor as 'deformity converted into beauty, and a nuisance rendered a picturesque accessory', it provides a lasting challenge to the modernist notion that in the design of a building form is determined by function.

Sewage

It has been said that the best measure of civilisation is the distance man puts between himself and his sewage. By that standard, Perth did very badly until quite recently. As the Lade ceased to be used for a water supply it was used more routinely for carrying away sewage. The date of the first sewers is not accurately known but the local authority water records refer to proposals in the 1870s to extend the system at York Place, Dovecoteland and Claypotts and these no doubt were to be connections to a rudimentary system in the town itself. The general view is that the first sewer was probably in High Street and the records at the end of the nineteenth century clearly show an outfall directly into the Tay at the junction of High Street and Tay Street. A further source of gross pollution— but good fishing—was the outfall from the slaughterhouse at Shore Road. In the present climate of concern for the environment, it is sobering to think that, until the present sewage works at Sleepless Inch were opened in 1971, all of the city's raw sewage was released directly into the river, which was perhaps a suitable riposte to Dundee for their impudent proposal to lower the rail bridge at the mouth of the Tay. The procedure involved storage in tanks at a point south of the Harbour and release into the river on an ebb tide which, through mis-timing or tricks of Nature, could lead to the presence along the Tay Street frontage of what the Burgh Surveyor's records used to describe as 'gross floatables' .

Living Conditions

Some idea of the working conditions can be imagined from this 1890 photo of the Sewing Room of Campbell's Dye Works which was subsequently taken over by Pullars.

Improvement to the water supply and sanitation arrangements continued throughout the Victorian period and, important as they were, they did not resolve the public health issue. Overcrowding was, in itself, increasingly recognised as a cause of disease and in a series of Public Health Acts, commencing in 1848, standards began to be introduced which affected living conditions and, in

particular, how new buildings and streets should be laid out. This public health legislation was the direct forerunner to the first Planning Act in 1947 which brought with it the concept of 'zoning', leading to the physical separation of residential environments from the industrial uses with which previously they had been completely intermixed. Some idea of the density of development and the mixing of what we would now regard as incompatible uses can be gained from looking at the 1860 Ordnance Survey maps. At that time Pullars in Mill Street was employing some 2,000 people cheek by jowl with residential areas; there was a gasworks in Canal Street (another of Adam Anderson's creations) and there was a diverse mixture of foundries, breweries and mills of various descriptions. An equally striking feature from those same maps is the sheer number of pubs and churches which may suggest that the inhabitants spent equal time trying to forget their living conditions in this world and preparing for the next. In 1837 there were 323 sales outlets for ale and spirits.

Pullar's Works which employed 2,000 workers in the heart of the city beside tenement housing, a gas works and other industries including a tannery in the nineteenth and early twentieth century. This photograph was taken in 1981.

If these conditions were also a cause of recurrent need for medical attention it might explain another of Soutar's verses written in the 1940s:

> *Wha daunders round St Johnstoun,*
> *Or up and doun onie gate,*
> *Will gang by monie a kirk and pub,*
> *And monie a doctor's plate.*

It is difficult now to imagine the problem that families in cramped conditions had in maintaining the basic decencies of life without an internal water supply.

In July 1845 the Town Council had received a petition from the Committee of the Working Classes requesting a grant of money to erect public baths over the Lade between Methven Street and the Union Bridge. In the spirit which has accompanied all major development issues in Perth from the date of the suggested railway terminus on the South Inch to the proposed demolition of the City Hall and more recent city expansion options, there followed a period of controversy with alternative sites being suggested and disquiet about the technical feasibility of the scheme. A section of the community felt that if placed in Mill Street the baths would 'spoil the square' and a report in the *Perth Courier* in January 1846 suggested that the middle classes might not take advantage of the baths in that location. They were constructed in that year, however, and whether through reservations about the appearance of the building, or scepticism about the benefits of personal cleanliness, patronage was regarded as disappointing by the authorities and there was a danger of financial collapse until, in 1857, a wash-house was built. An explanation for the different levels of usage may be found in the fact that the charges for a bath ranged from 1/6d (marble bath) to 4d (third class) whereas the washing and drying department charged 2d per hour for the first hour for each person and 1d per hour thereafter.

The popularity of the wash-house with the townswomen led, in 1902, to the construction of a new wash-house on the site of the old gasworks in Canal Street with the aid of a major grant from Sir Robert and Lady Pullar. These fall within my own memory. I can clearly remember being transported, once a week, to the Canal Street/Charles Street wash-house on top of a pyramid of laundry in an old pram. Thousands of other children made the same journey, which could best be compared to travelling on a three legged camel with a limp hump. These facilities naturally declined in popularity with the increased ownership of domestic washing machines and they were finally demolished in 1970.

It was unusual for houses, particularly in the town centre, to have internal facilities for laundry or even personal bathing until after the Second World War. The first public wash house and laundry was provided at Mill StreetMurray Street in the mid nineteenth century.

Tending the Sick

Before the Reformation in 1560 it was an honoured function of the monasteries and other religious institutions to care for the poor and infirm. Some were actually founded expressly for that purpose.

In the thirteenth century twelve religious orders existed in the burgh and by the later Middle Ages there were three friaries, five hospitals and a nunnery. It can be assumed therefore that the sick and poor were not completely neglected in those times.

In medieval times there was a hospital for lepers on the east bank of the Tay within what was known as the Lipper-croft. The exact location of the hospital or the Rood Chapel associated with it is not known but it was on and around the area presently occupied by the Potterhill Flats.

After the Reformation it was decreed that revenues formerly accruing to religious houses should be set aside for schools, hospitals and other godly purposes so that during the reign of Mary Queen of Scots several hospitals were established in Scottish towns.

Perth's King James VI Hospital was, as its name implies, founded by her son through a charter which directed that the endowments (financed by income from the former chapels and monasteries) be administered by the kirk session on behalf of the poor, maimed and distressed persons, orphans and for other pious or divine purposes. Its first location seems to have been in, or on the site of, the High Street where the Old council chambers now stand. The completed building was three storeys high and was operating in 1598.

The building was destroyed in 1651 by Cromwell's soldiers, along with the walls and tombstones of Greyfriars Cemetery and over 140 dwellings, and the stone used to build a citadel on the South Inch. For a period of 100 years thereafter there was no dedicated hospital building until the present building was erected at what is now known as Hospital Street but was formerly the lands of the Carthusian Monastery. Spanning the functions of what would now be known as health care, social work, education and the prison service, the new building housed a charity school, a reformatory, an infirmary, a correction house and a poor's house.

For many years the hospital was successful in performing the duties set out in its charter but early in the nineteenth century maintaining the building became a problem and the poor were reluctant to take refuge in a place which had the stigma of being 'The Poor's House'. In 1814 the hospital manager decided to place the residents on what was described as 'an outside footing' whereby they were allowed to take their beds and bedding and were given £12.00 each per year.

The County and City Infirmary was built in York Place between 1834 and 1836, close to the King James VI Building, to a neo-classical design by the city architect of the day, WM Mackenzie, and is probably the most important of the many buildings he designed in and around Perth. At the time, the location was criticised as being entirely inappropriate because it was too far from the centre of the city and therefore inconvenient for patients and visitors. The smile which this might bring to the face of some readers may be short-lived if they remember that, less that five years ago, a similar criticism was made when it was said that it was too far from the Centre to be a replacement for the Sandeman Library.

The York Place building closed as a hospital in 1914 when the new Perth Royal Infirmary was built and subsequently expanded in many phases. It is now an exemplary focal point for medical services in the whole of Perth and Kinross—an area of some 2000 square miles—and a source of pride and reassurance to the 140,000 people who live there. It is ironic, in fact, outrageous, that after 1,500 years of growth and prosperity, the local tradition of medical care for the community is under threat by medical authorities elsewhere threatening to remove many of the hospital's functions to Dundee.

Slum Clearance, Public Housing and Rising Living Standards

In the same way that public health legislation at the end of the nineteenth century gave rise to what subsequently became known as 'town planning', it also led to a series of acts which propelled local authorities into the role of being large scale providers of housing. The concerns which led to this responsibility are well summed up in the following extract from the King's Speech to representatives of the Local Authorities in 1919:

> While the housing of the working classes has always been a question of the
> greatest social importance, never has it been so important as now. It is not
> too much to say that an adequate solution of the housing question is the
> foundation of all social progress. . . . The first point at which the attack
> must be delivered is the unhealthy, ugly, overcrowded house in the mean
> street, which all of us know too well. If a healthy race is to be reared, it
> can be reared only in healthy homes; if drink and crime are to be
> successfully combated, decent, sanitary houses must be provided; if 'unrest'
> is to be converted into contentment, the provision of good houses may
> prove one of the most potent agents in that conversion.

Until World War I there was never any doubt that the private builder would continue to meet all normal housing needs and if local authorities had any role at all it would be in the provision of accommodation for families displaced by sanitary improvement schemes. As the War itself demanded ever greater sacrifices from the population, a commitment on the part of the Government to major social reforms came to constitute the other side of an unwritten social contract which acknowledged that modern war could only be endured if it held out the prospect of a better world and a better life for its survivors. The coalition Government of Lloyd George enshrined this attitude in the phrase 'Homes fit for Heroes' which was both a rallying cry and an election promise. In 1918 the Tudor Walters Committee produced a report drawing on the early experience of model towns and the garden city movement which in turn drew on concepts of planning developed by Ebeneezer Howard, Raymond Unwin and others who, at the beginning of the twentieth century, translated the theory into practice in places like Letchworth and Welwyn.

The Tudor Walters Report, published in 1918, explicitly stated that its purpose was to 'profoundly influence the general standard of housing in this country', and to encourage the building of houses of such quality that they would remain above the acceptable minimum standard for at least 60 years. It not only set standards for the size and number of rooms to be incorporated in generously sized 'model' house types but also recommended a maximum density of 12 houses to the acre in towns (8 in the country). The low densities were intended to provide families with more air, light and garden space. A fear of social unrest and the spread of Bolshevism alluded to in the King's Speech persuaded all political parties of the urgent need to implement these recommendations and a massive housing programme followed the approval of the 1919 and 1924 Housing Acts. The first example of housing in Perth which resulted from this movement is at Darnhall Drive which, stylistically, is very much of the type illustrated in the contemporary Housing Manual for local authorities describing the terms on which Government grants would be available.

Despite a strong industrial tradition throughout the nineteenth century in dyeing, spinning, distilling, railways, ironfounding and even shipbuilding no large areas of tenements had been built in Perth but under the new Acts and subsequent Housing Slum Clearance (Scotland) Act, 1930, the Council embarked on a major programme of public sector housing which was fully reviewed in a *Perthshire Advertiser* article dated 8 February 1933. It pointed out that skilled workmen taking up residence in the town experienced much more difficulty in finding a dwelling-place than a job:

> That is not a good advertisement for Perth—were new industries to be secured, as it is hoped they will be, where are the workers to be housed?

The article states that in the preceding twelve years the Council had constructed 786 houses in places which, apart from Darnhall Drive, included Stanley Place, Eviot Crescent, Gray Street, Needless Road, Crieff Road, Dunkeld Road, Florence Place, Riggs Road, Jeanfield Road and a major scheme of 108 houses at Friarton. The article refers to the Council's future ambitions to continue the programme under forthcoming legislation but points out that the task ahead is so large that the Council cannot do it alone and the private builder must be brought into action with a sentence that proved to be remarkably prescient:

> There are signs of a growing demand for suburban residences of the bungalow type.

The private sector quickly agreed with this assessment and, in 1933, the Burgh Surveyor of the period, Thomas MacLaren, reported to the first Scottish National Housing and Town Planning Committee's Conference in the City Chambers in May 1933 that:

> There has been a considerable amount of ribbon development along public roads but this had almost reached a stage when those contemplating the erection of houses would not be relieved of street works and would be compelled to utilise the remaining land that was available. Speculative builders had now almost exhausted vacant ground fronting the roads and were reluctant to build new houses on account of the additional cost of street works.
>
> Ribbon building upon public roads had hampered the proper development of some lands in that no proper provision had been made for streets joining up the thoroughfares already formed.

This led him to the conclusion that, since only 662 acres of the total burgh area of 3,162 acres were undeveloped, 'little required to be done in town planning except regulating the layout of these spaces between streets already formed'. The principal needs were 'to secure a more logical and coherent expansion of building development than would be the case were the location of proposed buildings left entirely to fortuitous circumstances'.

The relocation of Perth Academy from Rose Terrace to Viewlands in 1932 gave a considerable boost to expansion in Burghmuir and by December 1934 Mr McLaren was reporting in the *Perthshire Constitutional and Journal*:–

... notable changes are seen all over the Burghmuir district. Street improvements have been followed by building developments at Goodlyburn and Burghmuir Road. The reconstruction of Viewlands Road, Fairies Road and Oakbank Road has resulted in desirable residences springing up with astonishing rapidity. The new Academy will soon be within a built up area.

Perth's first council houses were built at Darnhall Drive in the 1920s as a result of the 1919 and 1924 Housing Acts. The process continued until the 1980s in step with the clearance and modernisation of the older stock. By 1981, 66 per cent of the total housing stock was provided by the Council.

The large housing schemes in Pitheavlis and Darnhall areas, as well as at Friarton, Dunkeld and Crieff Roads, form new suburbs where people who lived in congested districts are now housed in healthy and comfortable surroundings.

In the centre of the city the largest is seen in and around the new Art Galleries and Museums. The old houses in Castle Gable and Bridge Lane have been demolished and these streets widened. This improvement, with the lifting of the tram rails and the re-paving of George Street, will alter the whole aspect of the area, and make an attractive centre, in place of the drab and squalid buildings which recently stood there. The widening of the Castle Gable at the Horse Cross will provide a much needed Parking Place for cars and improve the junction of this space with Mill Street.

In the same article he makes a reference to the Tay Street shelters which in recent times were regarded more ambivalently because of less sociable uses being made of them.

> The shelters erected in Tay Street have proved a source of great pleasure to old and young when using this beautiful promenade in the summer months, and during inclement weather they are greatly appreciated. The design has been favourably commented on and does not detract from the pleasant appearance of the embankment.

The gem of the private sector housing of this period was the Gannochy development which was reviewed under the heading 'Our Sunshine Suburb' in a *Perthshire Advertiser* article of 8 February 1933 as follows:–

> No better monument to private enterprise, or greater impetus to individual endeavour, could be found than Perth's 'Sunshine Suburb'. Less than two years ago Messrs. Arthur Bell & Sons completed their ambitious private housing scheme of 150 houses at Gannochy.
>
> The proprietors insisted on all the houses being given a southern exposure to secure the maximum sunlight and this has been given effect by the architects—Messrs. Smart, Stewart & Mitchell.
>
> It was of Gannochy that the Chancellor of the Exchequer (Mr Neville Chamberlain) said: 'I have visited many housing schemes but this one is unique in character, and certainly the best I have ever seen'.

Private sector contribution to the need for housing after the First World War. A model scheme of 150 houses built by Arthur Bell and Sons at Gannochy and described as Perth's Sunshine Suburb.

The Second World War brought a temporary end to this progression but, like its predecessor, gave fresh impetus to it with reforming post-war legislation

including the 1947 Planning Act. Local authority schemes became even larger in conception—Letham, Tulloch and North Muirton leading through the 1950s and 1960s to a clear dominance of local authority housing over other forms of tenure. By 1971 only 29.5 per cent of city households had 'owner occupied' homes but this proved to be a turning point since, in line with national policy, public sector programmes were drastically reduced through that decade and the private sector was increasingly seen as the principal provider of homes. Most of this occurred in an almost uninterrupted sweep westwards, over a period of some 20 years, from Fairies Road to the Western Bypass.

Most of that development, loosely known at the 'Western Edge', took place on some 340 acres (138 ha) of what was once common land and known as the 'burgh muir'. This was acquired by the town in the fifteenth century from William, Lord Ruthven and during the seventeenth century it was leased to various individuals. The earliest surviving lease is dated 1673 and states that the muir was of no profit to the town so it was rented out to one John Lambe 'lest the borrow moor should return to its primitive baroness'. Under the lease he was entitled to remove broom and grass, enclose, sublet, cultivate and manure parts of it and build on it. The people of Perth retained the right to take turf to repair the roofs of their houses.

In 1714 the Council decided to plant the muir with trees on the basis that they 'may prove profitable and pleasant'. The Provost bought 14,000 young Scots pines and Alexander Reid ' ane old qualified gardener' was employed to supervise the planting.

In 1719 the town received the first income from the project and planting continued despite some protracted disputes with the Duke of Atholl over boundaries between his land and the muir. As the trees matured, townspeople could acquire a cartload of wood for 5 shillings although it seems that many found themselves in court because of their reluctance to do things officially. In *Traditions of Perth* George Penny records that by the 1830s the Burgh Muir was 'intersected by fine avenues, which formed delightful walks in the summer season'. Maps of the period show that the plantation was the largest in the area. At its centre was a large clearing from which radiated eight avenues.

In 1773 the Council appointed three further muir keepers who were to be 'stout and able bodied men of honest character' and the regulations stated that, together with the one previously appointed, 'they shall go through the planting with gun and dog and seize and bring before the magistrates any suspicious persons they find there'.

Throughout its life the plantation consisted mainly of Scots pine and oak but there were also some elm and sycamore which were transplanted to line the avenues of the North and South Inches at the end of the eighteenth century.

For the best part of 100 years the Council's coffers benefited from the sale of timber from the muir but re-investment seemed to be lacking and in 1796 a land surveyor was appointed to give an opinion on its future use. This resulted in the whole muir being disposed of in 1804.

The small enclave of Woodlands is all that now remains as a reminder of a once impressive forest but as a place name—together with Oakbank and Burghmuir—it will keep alive some memory of a previous century.

The private housing estates which have occurred on, and around, the muir have played a major part in raising the level of owner occupied housing in the city to 34.7 per cent in 1981 and 52.7 per cent in 1991 (the date of the most recent census).

Population Trends and Influences

The first truly reliable census was carried out on a national basis in 1801, at which time the Perth burgh population was 14,878 and, except in war time, there has beem a census every ten years thereafter. All other historical estimates are of dubious reliability but a thesis written by Peter Vasey in 1987 suggests that immediately after the burgh was constituted, probably in 1120, it may have contained around 500 inhabitants. By 1562 it may have grown to 6,000 but progress between those dates was not steady because periods of high mortality caused by national disasters, plague and war frequently depleted the population. The flood of 1209 which destroyed both the bridge and castle left many plots barren because, in all probability, their owners had perished. In 1244 Perth was one of eight burghs accidentally destroyed by fire and in 1385 it was burned a second time, on this occasion by the English.

The earliest reference to the population of Perth being affected by the plague was in 1335 when the disease was said to have killed almost a third of the inhabitants. It struck again on many occasions in the sixteenth century, killing 1,427 people in the 1584–85 outbreak. Mr Vasey's account suggests that, by the early decades of the seventeenth century, the population of Perth had fallen to around 5,000, partly as a result of plagues but also because of famines such as those of 1602–3 and 1615–16.

With such a catalogue of disasters it is easy to regard them as a series of dates and overlook the full horror and misery they caused but, set against the shock of our own flood of 1993, consider the following contemporary account of the inundation of 1621 which led to the bridge collapse:

> Befoir xii of the clocke the nycht all the peopill in the castle gavill and west port wer wat in their beddis and wakened with water to the waist in their flooris. It seemit the windowis of heavin and fountaines of the dep were opponit. It carried away the ellewin bow brig of Tay. It was within one fute in hecht from the crose of Perth. It tuike doon the gawill of the tolbuith. This it did in the common streit of the town be divers and manie menes losses. The peopill of the castlegavill had diet, about iii hundred soules, gif a buatt hed nott bein borne be men from the spey tour to it. God lett us never sie the eillik of it againe.

In the same year, storms and ice ruined the harvest and, in the year after, typhus ravaged the area when it was recorded that 'noe familie in all the citie wes frie of this visitation'. As always, these disasters weigh most heavily on the poor and a further harvest failure in 1623 again caused 'ane great mortalitie and death so that x or xii diet ordanarilie everie day from midsommer to mychelmas'. On this occasion perhaps 2,000 died, many of them recently arrived vagrants from the Highlands driven to Perth by a desperate need for food.

In the winter of 1623–24 the Tay was frozen from mid-November to the end of January and again in February. In 1634 it snowed almost continuously from 26 January to 16 February, lying 6 feet deep throughout the burgh. The Tay was frozen for about a month and there was 'great skairstie of victuall'.

In the mid 1640s bubonic plague returned to Perth and, while this was the last major outbreak of the disease in Scottish history, it was, in Perth's case, the most severe resulting in possibly some 3,000 deaths.

To break the pattern of harsh winters Nature showed her versatility by visiting severe drought and 'great heate' in 1652 as another means of causing food shortages and hardship.

In parallel with disease and crop failures, the economy had suffered as a result of loss of national status when its political and religious significance declined. By the end of the thirteenth century no less than twelve religious houses held or owned land in the burgh and Parliament regularly met there until the assassination of James I in the Blackfriars Monastery in 1437 led to the withdrawal of the royal court. The trade which had flourished during the early medieval period declined as other ports—particularly on the Clyde—grew in importance. The long-established trade with Holland fell dramatically during the seventeenth century because of the Anglo-Dutch Wars and, in 1672, the abolition of the near-monopoly trading privileges previously enjoyed by all burghs also had an adverse effect.

All of these factors suggest, from Mr Vasey's analysis of Hearth and Poll Tax returns, that the population of Perth was probably around 5,000 at the close of the seventeenth century and that, economically, politically and demographically, the town reached its nadir in the third quarter of that period, all of which had a negative effect on population growth.

By the middle years of the eighteenth century three separate estimates referred to by Mr Vasey suggest that the population had increased to between 6,060 and 9,019. The most reliable of these, commissioned by the Magistrates of Perth, indicated 7,542 inhabitants, which occurred due to natural increase, inward migration and a period largely free from the pestilence, famine and general hardship of the previous century. To be sure, the Kirk session and Council records continued to show substantial numbers of poor people receiving relief and in 1707 it is recorded that Perth was beset by 'ane great manie vagrant persons that creep into this place' and legislation was introduced to prevent the poor begging door to door.

The population of the burgh at each census date since 1851 is shown below from which it can be seen that there has been a regular increase with the exception of the period which spanned the First World War and in the 1971 to 1991 period when a large proportion of new development was taking place in the surrounding villages and there was a marked drop in the average household size.

1851 – 23,835	1861 – 25,293	1871 – 25,606
1881 – 28,980	1891 – 29,919	1901 – 32,873
1911 – 33,807	1921 – 33,208	1931 – 34,807
1951 – 40,487	1961 – 41,196	1971 – 42,344
1981 – 41,918	1991 – 41,490	

If present planning policy is continued future growth of the city itself will be curtailed to avoid in-filling important green spaces or spreading beyond the logical boundaries set by the bypass and the natural urban setting. The principal focus of further development will be at the new villages of Almond Valley and Oudenarde with approximate potential for 1,000 houses and associated community uses at each location. A third option involving a new village at Errol comprising some 2,000 houses is also under consideration.

Our disappointment that more of Old Perth has not survived has to be tempered with consideration for the conditions of the people who lived there. This photograph dating from the 1870s shows an area known as Shuttlefield Close which was being demolished prior to the construction of Scott Street.

Back to the future

Personal observations on what has been lost— and might be gained

Lo! what was old is passed away,
And all things are made new!

shaped by at least 1500 years of human settlement. Throughout that period it has been under almost continuous change and the process will continue for as long as people wish to live here and adapt the city to their circumstances.

It is tempting to look back for a 'golden age' when it would have been at its best or, according to our individual tastes, it would have looked its best. To many people perhaps that might be found at the end of the medieval period as depicted in the first print of 1693.

At any time from then until 1766 it would have had a wall and, if frozen in that state, it would no doubt be an architectural and planning gem that would bear comparison with the fortified Bastide towns of Southern France. But if its growth had been arrested at that point we would have been denied the classical splendours of Marshall Place and Rose Terrace which attracted the enthusiastic description given by Dr Dibdin in 1837.

The truth probably is that if the city at all its stages of evolution were laid out for examination like exhibits in a show case, most of us would choose a version dating from before the middle of the nineteenth century. Whether we would have found it comfortable to live in is a different matter.

The charge that successive generations of city fathers have recklessly thrown away our urban heritage is a recurrent one which was very well expressed in 1914 in an article under the heading 'Auld Perth'.

> The citizens of Perth have been often foolish enough to exchange old lamps for new ones, which, however valuable and useful they may be in themselves, they do not seem to light up our past history. The authorities gave up and demolished Gowrie House for a jail. Many were favourable to the surrender of the South Inch for a Railway Station. All that remained of St Mary's Chapel—perhaps the oldest Christian foundation in Perth—was swept away in our time to make a clear space for the Municipal Buildings. This beautiful pile, built in the Tudor-Gothic style, is an ornament to the city; yet we cannot but regret that again an old historic lamp has been extinguished.

Since those words were written other precious buildings have been lost, such as the former Post Office at the corner of Scott Street and High Street. If there is a single explanation, it is that town planning in Perth, and nationally, has been driven by the need to improve the living conditions of the majority of citizens who until the first Housing Acts of the 1920s did not have, and could not be given, decent living standards under their existing roofs. A look at the photograph of Shuttlefield Close illustrates the point. In words, William Soutar captured the social conditions in areas like Shuttlefield Close and Ropemaker's Close with the following lines from his poem 'Backlands'.

> *In backlands aff the Ropey Close,*
> *Whan the mune grows cauld and sneep,*
> *The bairnies wha were beddit boss*
> *Hae grat themsel's to sleep.*
>
> *The auld wife, boo'd abune her wark,*
> *Steeks on be cannel-flame:*
> *The sma'-hour dinnles through the dark;*
> *The trollop taivers hame.*

In response to these conditions there was, therefore, a strong 'clear and build' philosophy in the immediate post–war period which was maintained by at least three factors:–

(1)   The local sandstone used throughout the eighteenth and nineteenth centuries was soft, porous and often laid at right angles to its natural 'bed' so that layers tended to spall or peel away from the weathered face. The structural walls often did not, therefore, provide a shell worth reusing and, equally, the use of Dunkeld slate, although cheap, did not have long term resistance to rain.

(2)   Improvements or new construction carried out by successive Councils relied upon Central Government grants which, from the earliest times, had stringent 'cost yardsticks' against which new build options invariably triumphed over rehabilitation. The annual number of new houses built was a source of pride—and an electoral issue—for successive post war Governments and Councils.

(3)   By and large the people who lived in cramped, insanitary conditions favoured a clean break to a new house with, for many, the first chance of a private garden.

But, as always in civic matters, the arguments are not one-sided. Having worked in town planning in Perth since 1968 it is a great embarrassment to me that in the same period so many fine buildings have been lost. Many of them were not at the end of their structural life or in need of demolition to create healthy living conditions—and if they were, did not deserve to be replaced by buildings of such indifferent quality.

My own, entirely personal, explanation for the mistakes—or lost opportunities—is that we have paid a high price for the influence of the motor vehicle—which was inevitable—and modernistic architecture, which was not. In civic design terms, the consequences of both factors is most worrying in the town centre which, like most town centres, is where one looks for a defining quality and identity. It is also where most of the things worth preserving were located.

In that area there is hardly a building dated before the second World War which seems 'out of place'. This can be explained, I think, by the fact that until then architects looked, by training and instinct, to inherited styles for their inspiration but the post war architectural (and planning) consensus has grouped around modernist ideals. To call them ideals is in fact stretching the point since they were very much the result of short-term fashion based on self expression, nudged by technological innovations in building practice and materials. What was technically possible to some extent became obligatory and to argue against this trend became 'non-progressive'. With the distinguished exception of the AK Bell Library all post war civic building (in particular) has been driven by the 'let's do something modern' call. Examples of this are the 1950s Pomarium and Potterhill flats (outside the centre but linked visually to it), the 1960s Market Street flats, the 1970s Leonard Street flats and Post Office, the 1980s Police Headquarters, the Canal Street car park and now the new car park behind Pullar House. In each of these there are hardly any recognisable features, reference points in design or commonality of friendly materials which establish the building's lineage in a local tradition. Yet this is part of the respect which new buildings should pay to the old. It knits them into their surroundings as opposed to being stand-alone pieces of architecture where self expression and technical innovation rather than neighbourliness is the primary concern.

North Side of Canal Street, in 1875, before formation of Scott Street.

North Side of South Street, in 1875, before formation of Scott St.

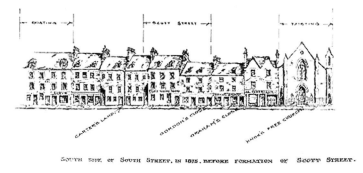

South Side of South Street, in 1875, before formation of Scott Street.

Elevation drawings from Council records showing South Street before Scott Street was formed towards the end of the nineteenth century. Individually, the buildings are designed in a simple vernacular style with each intended to 'fit in' rather than clamouring to make a statement in some new fashion. The result was harmonious and more pleasing to the eye than the South Street left by the twentieth century.

The Modern Movement gained its suffocating grip on 2,500 years of architectural practice immediately after the Second World War when many of its east European pioneers found their way into teaching posts in architectural schools and there was an influx of students being released from the armed forces with an idealistic zeal to build a new Britain. One of these, who was subsequently hailed as 'a genius' of the movement, was Jim Stirling who is quoted in his biography as saying:

Back to 1946—end of a war is always a start of something. The cities were bombed and devastated. From now on, everything could only be better. We assumed that from here on everything would be built as Modern Architecture. In the schools of this time, the rightness of modern as against past styles was not even debated; the overpowering logic of modern architecture was completely accepted, and the pioneering stage was over.

His biographer goes on to make my point even more helpfully:

Any imitation of past styles, or use of the ornamental language associated with them, was taboo. The form and treatment of a building should derive immediately from its function, without reference to the past (the possibility that one of its functions might be to refer to the past was never considered). Ornament of any kind was suspect; it was a way of concealing absence of thought. Even architects whose buildings were carefully contrived for aesthetic reasons tended to talk or write as though the design of their buildings derived in some kind of inevitable way from their functions.

. . . Any suggestion that the Modern Movement was just another new
style of building was anathema. They were escaping from style. They had
discovered not one way of building but the right way of building.'

The hostility to ornamentation and the 'form follows function' notion are two of
modernism's core beliefs. As the above quotation illustrates, it was asserted
that the form, or appearance, of a building had to emerge inexorably from its
function—in other words be designed from the inside out with the external
considerations being subordinate to functional requirements. Both of these
notions are complete nonsense which is fortunate since, increasingly, buildings
last longer than their functions and may change their use every few years. The
truth is, in fact, that the most successful buildings are those which are *least*
attached to their initial function and most able to survive a change. Evidence of
this is all around us in the town centre: Adam Anderson's Water works became
offices then an art gallery; the Lower City Mills were refurbished to create craft
workshops then offices; the Upper City Mills became a hotel; the County Hospital
in York Place became offices then a library; the conversion of the Middle Church
to a workshop, then warehouse then flats and, most recently, the Pullars laundry
and dye works became a supermarket then new Council offices.

Unfortunately both of the above theories have become embedded in
architectural patter by unquestioning repetition—like oaths in a playground—
and have done a great deal of damage since they were first uttered in the early
twentieth century. Precious historic areas demand that form is actually more
important than function and, if the two considerations cannot be reconciled in
the design process, it is function that must give way.

After a short, but too long, life modernism was superseded by 'post
modernism' which attempted to overcome the charmless, soulless austerity of
what has been built so far by introducing embellishment but it does so using
historical details in a flippant uncomprehending way. In an authentic style there
is continuity between structure and decoration—in post modernism decoration
is invariably a crude 'add-on'.

It is also striking that, in Perth, the modernist buildings I have mentioned
lack coherence not only with their surroundings but also with each other because
of the dual influences of the urge for self expression by their designers and
frequent changes in architectural fashion over that fifty year post war period.
By comparison, in a similar span of fifty years in the nineteenth century, the
elegant terraces from Charlotte Street to Rose Terrace developed harmoniously
with each new phase showing exemplary respect to its neighbours.

Hindsight is, of course, always more acute than foresight and it would
undoubtedly have been difficult to reconcile post war space standards, changing
building practice, the political will for maximum housing numbers and a constant
exhortation for low cost solutions with the conservation interest which was
regarded as rather eccentric until recently.

The cost argument is a particularly pernicious one coming, as it does, from
both the public and private sector. It is used in pre-development discussions,
often in a tactical way, to fend off demands for design changes for more suitable
finishing materials which, the clients say, will put the viability and time-scale of
the project at risk. The correct response would be to say to the proposers that if
they do not have the resources to put up a suitable building they cannot afford it
but when this card is played the usual scenario is for 'the planners' to be portrayed
as unreasonable and the ones who are putting a much-needed project at risk

through their obduracy. The planners, for their part, feel uncomfortable in this role especially when they believe that the Council attaches greater importance to other issues.

These arguments took a new and depressing turn at the design stage for the new multi-storey car park at Carpenter Street. Aluminium cladding panels were proposed, and used, not merely because they were cheaper than more friendly materials but because they would require minimal maintenance and 'would not age'. Since buildings became part of the fabric of a town through the ageing process that is a promise which, if true, will separate this structure from its neighbours as surely as the original, inappropriate, choice of materials, plucked from the nightmare of Milton Keynes..

Our predecessors had a need for economy which was as great, and arguably greater, than ours but in many ways they behaved with greater civic responsibility. It is hard to imagine the minutes of any current project committee—public or private sector—matching the concern of the hospital authority when it was considering the erection of a lodge house beside the County and City Infirmary which was built in 1834–1836 at York Place.

> The original design of the House was submitted in 16 April 1836. It was soon seen that the erection of a lodge for the Porter was indispensable and that its position was necessarily at the principal Gate of Admission. So anxious were the Directors to study economy that it was proposed by many of them, to place the lodge at the back gate, but it appeared to the majority, that to be really useful, its position behoved to be where the public would approach the building, and that an opposite decision would involve a sacrifice of efficiency to economy. Having thus resolved on the erection of the building it became necessary, to avoid the censure of every person of taste, that the design should in style harmonise with the elegance of the principal building. This edifice cost much more than was at first expected, but, admitting the necessity of the erection, the Directors feel little fear of disapprobation on account of its style and consequent cost. They are satisfied that the whole outward appearance of the Building is such as confers credit on the County and City. Beyond this they are hopeful that the cheerful elegance and inviting taste, displayed all around, will do much to dispel vulgar prejudices against taking the benefits of the Institution. And further, they are confident that a Public Institution, seeking public support, should not be kept in concealment but should stand forward of the public gaze, as an object deserving and commanding attention, and pleading as for itself the support of the community.

One optimistic sign against a growing background of environmental concern, is that the public have been to some extent ahead of their politicians and officials as I find from the unsolicited opinions I receive about what has been built in place of the old. Despite the fact that architecture is the most public form of art, public opinion has been excluded for too long from the development process by the belief that while it is perfectly proper for the public to participate in decisions about what type of development should take place, and where it should take place, what that development should actually look like is a matter for debate only among a narrow group of designers, officials and councillors—many of whom are hesitant to express an opinion on this aspect of planning and, frankly, are more concerned with cost.

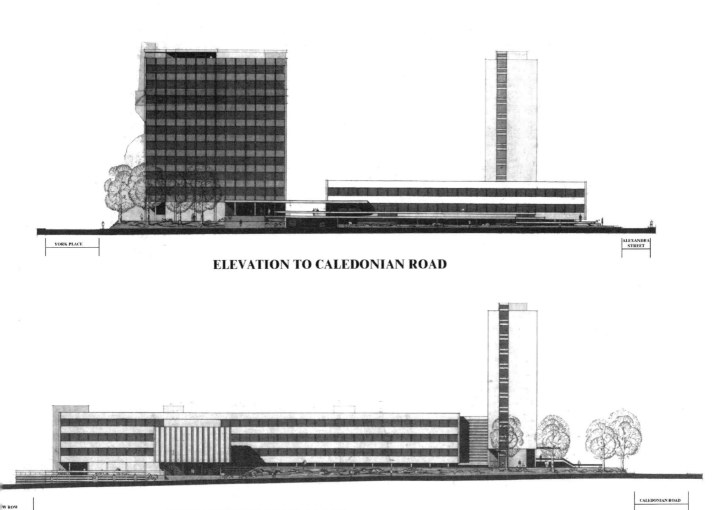

ELEVATION TO CALEDONIAN ROAD

ELEVATION TO YORK PLACE

We were spared this modernist nightmare which looks like a collision of the worst features of 1960s' civic architecture. This was a scheme designed by the County Council in the mid 1960s for local government offices rising to ten storeys. It would have required the demolition of the former County and City Infirmary (now part of the AK Bell Library) its gatehouse and the Caledonian Road primary school designed by Andrew Heiton and opened in 1892.

In lamenting what has been lost it is also too easy to overlook the important successes I have already mentioned in finding new uses for the former Water Works, the City Mills; the Middle Church, the AK Bell Library (and now the gatehouse), the restoration of Rose Terrace, the Fair Maid's House and a host of other listed buildings which have been given new life through the investment of the public and private sector. In terms of major new building, the St John's Centre elevation to King Edward Street has the style and dignity required for that location and is infinitely better than its 1950s predecessor. The current conversion of the former Pullars Works for Council Offices at Kinnoull Street/ Mill Street is also a major conservation success.

It will be evident from everything I have said above that my own leanings are towards a 'neo-historical' approach to civic design or, as the critics would label it, 'pastiche'—a term which is inherently disparaging and used by modernists to intimidate those of less sophisticated tastes. It is a word which, used properly, merely means 'a musical, artistic or literary work in someone else's style, or a mixture of styles.' But in current architectural circles it is always used as a jibe, repeated parrot-fashion, without any need to explain why a building designed in the style of someone else—or from another age—should be reprehensible. A moment's thought would show that the features which are most appreciated in Perth (and elsewhere) are largely designed 'out of period'. Looking no further than Tay Street, an attractive composition which developed incrementally through the nineteenth century, the Sheriff Court and the former waterworks are 'Neo Classical', the Old City Chambers 'Tudor Gothic', Gowrie House 'French Gothic' and elsewhere 'Teutonic Romanesque', 'Renaissance' and 'Thomsonian Greek'

Virtually all of the buildings in the statutory list of Buildings of Architectural and Historic interest for Perth have an equally diverse lineage and, by the modernists' use of the terms 'pastiche', would deserve to be condemned which of course they are not. Most European populations revere what is old in their built surroundings and re-create it—sometimes literally—as in the case of Warsaw and many war-damaged continental cities. They did this because culture and community identity are based on a sense of shared historical experience which is in part provided by our surroundings. It is also a fact that the most visited, admired and photographed destinations are precisely those towns and cities which have the most 'historical' ambience. You can wait a very long time to see a tourist in Cumbernauld, Glenrothes or any other 'new town'.

There are many flourishing examples of cities where twentieth century industrial and commercial growth has been accepted to create prosperity, but the historical centres have generally been preserved as a source of civic pride to their citizens and delight to visitors. Brussels, which is the focus of the European movement, is an obvious but far-from- rare example. The sentiment behind this practice has been summarised very well by Roger Scruton, a former Professor of Aesthetics at Birbeck College who said:

> Having achieved what we value, we wish to make it permanent, to cling to
> it, to make it one with ourselves. In most important things we strive for
> permanence.

In Perth we have thought it necessary (to the extent that we have thought about it at all) to give priority to other considerations in our town centre but we have weakened rather than ruined it: mistakes which are recognised are less likely to be repeated. Although the public, like many of their elected representatives, are not particularly at ease in expressing opinions on design issues, I hope it will be possible to distil some guiding principles for the next phase of development from a public consultation exercise on this topic alone. It would, I imagine, have to be done in a highly visual form portraying examples of past and recent buildings to establish characteristics which the local population admire and should therefore be incorporated in new buildings within the town centre. If, as I believe, the public view leans towards the 'neo historical' rather than modernist approach the basis for such design guidance might have been lying unnoticed in the recommendations of the former Burgh Surveyor and Planning Officer, WGS Murray who wrote the following in the early 1970s.

Streets and Architecture

> In the future the Centre will not be judged alone by its efficiency in terms
> of speed of transport or availability of a car park. It will also be measured
> by its architecture both old and new and to the extent that it reflects in all
> its possible richness the character of the town as a whole. It will be less, in
> this respect, on the success or failure of individual buildings that the centre
> will be accepted as on the overall effect of each street scene. Not all streets
> in the centre consist of buildings of a design worthy of preservation. But
> some contain amongst their older facades some buildings which are
> substantial and deserve to survive simply by that fact alone. Thus many of
> the main streets will be committed to a condition of partial but not
> complete rebuilding for some time to come. Very few streets will offer new

opportunities for complete rebuilding during this century. New building will need therefore to exist convincingly alongside and without detriment to much of the older examples. This situation demands a study and understanding of neighbouring buildings and the application to the facades of new building of the principles of the elements that comprise those adjacent. This approach is well removed from that which conceives the elevation of a building as a capricious amalgamation of whatever the floor plans demand and the designers' personal idiosyncrasies determine.

As each building presents its own problem there can be no universal rules on design for such streets. A successful result will likely embody the following principles, however:–

1. Building heights will conform fairly closely to those of neighbouring facades. The difference of more than a storey height is undesirable.
2. The frontages should be continuous.
3. The frontages should not embody long unbroken continuous elements. Units of facades over 30 feet in length will normally appear out of scale.
4. The design of elevations should neither be pronouncedly vertical nor horizontal in emphasis.
5. Materials of cheap appearance or colour are not likely to prove acceptable.
6. There is unlikely to be any place in the Central Area for building elevations employing proprietary mass produced units such as curtain walling.
7. Successful designs will likely rely on good proportion, sympathetic scale, subdued natural materials and elegance and poise in style. They will avoid employing materials simply because they are fashionable or design features because they are thought to belong to the current trend. Designers in the last resort should reject their own proposal if they feel that its introduction into a street will be outstandingly novel at first and plainly incongruous thereafter.

Preservation

The listed buildings should be retained as far as possible in their original form. The windows should be painted uniformly white. As these buildings were all originally houses, the residential character should be retained in their appearance, as far as possible, even if their use as houses no longer applies. Ostentatious commercial type signs and lettering are incompatible with the Georgian style.

Tay Street possesses an impressive terrace of handsome facades in stone to be preserved except near the south end where new buildings in a more fitting style is called for. The other main streets in the town where conservation of character, rather than preservation, is desirable, are High Street, George Street, King Street, St John's Street, St John's Place (North and South) and King Edward Street.

Mr Murray's words seem to me to provide excellent guidance for a historically faithful approach to future urban design. In an attempt to expand on them my own suggestions would be based on the following propositions.

• Perth's medieval connections can now be seen only in its central area street pattern. The medieval period offers no architectural pointers of any significance for future development.

- The 'best of Perth' in terms of urban townscape is to be found in the peripheral architecture of Marshall Place, Tay Street, Charlotte Street, Atholl Place and Rose Terrace which was grafted on to the town centre in the early nineteenth century. Within that ring what remains of earlier periods is of variable quality through being patched, altered and rebuilt piecemeal. There are, however, individual buildings and streets of genuine quality, notably St John Street and George Street.

- Of the two principal streets, High Street and South Street, High Street is more attractive and vibrant. South Street is mostly unattractive.

- Excluding modernist redevelopment since the Second World War, most of the town centre streets have two common features: strong, often well-detailed corner buildings linked by facades consisting of simple repeated patterns the best of which can be described as 'Artisan Georgian' and much of the remainder being harmoniously proportioned Victorian or Edwardian with strong classical references.

- The town centre lacks a proper civic space capable of holding markets, outdoor performances and festivals.

A sketch by the Belgian architect, Leon Krier, showing that harmonious urban design can be achieved by a limited number of high quality buildings, spaces and streets set within a background of unpretentious, but well executed, blocks.

Against that background I support a concept of urban form described by a Belgian architect, Leon Krier, which is illustrated very succinctly here. The bottom drawing is an illustration of a historic town and if you half close your eyes you could imagine it is an aerial view of our town centre. Above, in exploded form, are the two elements which contribute to a harmonious result—firstly the relatively few important buildings, civic spaces and streets which link them and, secondly, 'everything else'. The conclusion to be drawn is that it is not necessary for every building and space to make a strong statement. Provided they observe some basic architectural good manners it is enough that the majority provide a background setting for a much smaller number of truly important buildings and spaces. The facades which form the background group must, however, follow the guidance clearly set out by Mr Murray, shunning the inevitable pleas on grounds of cost or innovation to use modernist designs and materials. Harmony is not possible without composition and composition is not possible if the appearance of new buildings is subordinate to functional or cost considerations.

Krier's ideas could be applied to Perth through a hub and spoke network of attractive, pedestrian priority areas linking the St John's Kirk precinct (as the hub) with the river, the Horse Cross/Perth 2000 Concert and Conference Centre, the High Street and landmark buildings such as St Paul's Church, King James VI Hospital, Pullar House, AK Bell Library and the City Mills. At most of these locations and the links between them, there is a need for a programme of environmental improvements of a type which, with other

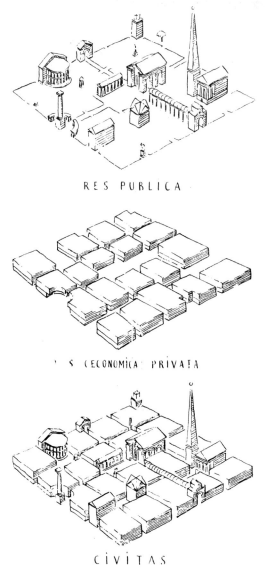

RES PUBLICA

' S (ECONOMICA PRIVATA

CIVITAS

With the re-opening of the Pullar building for Council offices and the new multi-storey car park behind it—followed, perhaps, by a new conference/concert hall at Horse Cross and new retail/commercial uses—the northern half of the city centre will become a more important pedestrian destination. Woolworths may well be demolished providing an opportunity for a new link in the form of another mall or, more adventurously, an arcade like the one in Leeds or the Galeria in Milan.

public sector officials, I was privileged to see recently in Lyons, a city which has transformed its image by attention to large and small scale public areas and, more adventurously, putting virtually all of their car parks underground.

I chose my words carefully in suggesting that the hub of this network should be the St John's Kirk precinct rather than 'the City Hall precinct'. In my view the City Hall, although understandably high in the affections of most Perth people, should be demolished to create an attractive civic square for the purposes I have already mentioned and a more suitable setting for our oldest and most venerated building, St John's Kirk. Such an opinion might seem hard to reconcile with the conservation views I have previously expressed but, in this case, there is every reason to believe that the town centre would gain more than it is losing.

The City Hall is not a building of any antiquity, it is oversized for the site—which was formerly a market square—and has become uneconomic to restore when set against the benefits of a new concert and conference building at the Horse Cross, through the Perth 2000 proposals. The replacement square could, however, be graced at its western end by the retention of the distinctive first section of the existing building incorporating the entrance from King Edward Street and the foyer area. Apart from providing enclosure for the square and a sense of historic continuity, the retained portion could serve a variety of civic, cultural or commercial purposes and on its reconstructed rear (east) elevation might incorporate a stage or podium for outdoor public performances. A prerequisite for any such partial demolition of the City Hall is of course the construction of a replacement facility which, although not yet certain, is becoming increasingly likely, in association with the new Council offices and commercial development in the Pullars building linked to High Street with new retailing opportunities through the clearance of the Woolworths site. To address the understandable criticism that the Perth shopping experience has increasingly become like that of our competitors, an attractive option would be to consider the construction of a roofed arcade which, at its most modest, would bear comparison with the Burlington in London, or at its most ambitious, with the Galeria in Milan which was the first of its type—and the most impressive.

Conclusion

The above opinions are entirely my own and I have no reason to believe that they will be shared by Perth and Kinross Council who are my present employers. From discussions I have had with Perth people and visitors throughout my working life, I do believe, however, that they chime with a majority public sentiment that too much of what was 'old' has been lost unnecessarily and too much of what has replaced it is discordant or, in plain words, ugly. If I am out of step with public opinion it will be most shockingly in relation to my views on the City Hall but, if that is the case, it may well prove my point. The affection which people have for that building is partly an appreciation of its classical architecture, partly esteem for its (assumed) age and partly community memories of entertainment and other life events shared by several generations. This could be condemned as nostalgia—but not by me—since that is to some degree the explanation of why, here and everywhere, people are comfortable in cities, towns and villages which have history and a respect for the patterns of the past in what is new. That proposition is certainly at the root of my own beliefs about what our town centre should be and, for the last word, I hand the page again to Roger Scruton who summarises the point far better than I ever could.

> Home is not only occupied by us: it is inhabited by the ghosts of our
> ancestors and by the premonition of children who are yet to be. Its essence
> is continuity, and it provides the archetype of every experience of peace.
>   The failings of modernism are to be witnessed less in its grandiose
> projects and striking novelties than in its patterns: the architectural
> elements that get into the hands of the talentless and uninstructed, and
> which repeated *ad nauseum* in every modern city, ensure that we find no
> resting place, but are everywhere homeless and insecure.

Mind our language, please

Plain, familiar words . . .

. . . well punctuated . . .

. . . with a strong ending . . .

. . . make an elegant sentence.

Bridgend. 1970s housing on a prominent riverside site facing the North inch. A style which has quickly dated showing no respect for the obvious classical reference points in the buildings to the north and at Rose Terrace on the other side of the river.

Richmond. Half-close your eyes and it could be the same river, same bridge, same site. A mixed residential and commercial development which was built in the 1990s but looks as if it has been there forever. Familiar features, modest scale, repeatable form and friendly materials but this and other work by the architect Quinlan Terry is vilified as 'pastiche' by the modernists.

Which do you prefer?

A SNOBBISH WORD

Pastiche is defined as a 'musical, artistic or literary work in someone else's style, or a mixture of styles'. In architecture it is always used as a disparaging term by modernists. Here are some examples of recent developments in Perth which have been dismissed as pastiche.

But do you like them?

GREEK AND LATIN WORDS

Our Georgian terraces and houses come in a direct line from ancient Greece and Rome via fifteenth century Renaissance Italy. For the next 500 years architects regarded classical styles as an inexhaustible source of inspiration for design and decoration but that practice was brought to an abrupt end in the mid twentieth century. Fortunately, a number of classically inspired buildings were constructed at the very end of the nineteenth century and they make an important contribution to the town centre not only because they are inherently attractive but also because they remind you that you are in Perth—and nowhere else. As you walk through town centre streets see how often the following classical features appear.

Columns and Pilasters, all five of the classical orders.

| *Tuscan* | *Doric* | *Ionic* | *Corinthian* | *Composite* |

Venetian windows

Pediments

Balustrades

Rusticated stone work

Cupolas

 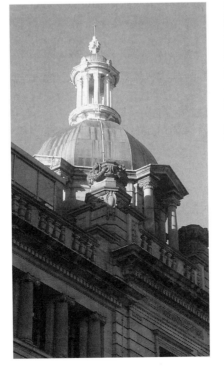 

Alfresco dining is a recent and highly successful import from continental Europe in the face of derisory predictions that it would be a flop. But at busy times the space is now barely adequate.

If the pavement in St John's Place were wider—or if a proper civic square were formed—a more 'continental' café quarter could be formed like this one in Lyons.

Similarly, the Farmer's Markets have been another recent success but because the space formerly available for these activities was lost at the beginning of the twentieth century when the City Hall was built on the Market Square, stalls now have to be strung along existing streets.

RUDE EXPRESSIONS

There are, at July 2000, 1,091 on-street parking spaces and 2,272 spaces in car parks within the town centre. Ideally, most of them would be underground but the construction cost per space for that sort of parking is eight to twelve times as great as for a surface level space. As in most British Cities, we have therefore put our main town centre parking in multi-storey car parks which cost only three to four times as much per space as surface level parking. Because of their size and function they are difficult to fit into the street scene but here are four recent attempts at addressing the problem. Which is the most pleasing to the eye?

Perth

Dundee

Glasgow

Stirling

The buildings which are most out of place in the town centre have all been built since the 1950s and have been prompted by the 'let's do something modern' urge with no respect for local traditions and materials.

The former Post Office at the corner of Scott Street and High Street. As well as being a landmark building with civic dignity in a Renaissance style, it was a much-loved meeting place.

The replacement Post Office in South Street is a 1970s creation with 1960s style flats above.

The 1950s Pomarium Flats. An alien form in a town centre of mainly three and four storey buildings, with an overbearing presence in an important conservation area.

TRIUMPH AND DISASTER

1990s extension at AK Bell Library incorporating classical features and materials sympathetic to the original 1834 building. The Market Street flats in the background were built in a 1960s style.

Police Station. Another 1970s/80s building in a 'here, there and everywhere' style.

The Market Street flats from Old High Street.

THE NEED FOR A CIVIC SQUARE

The lack of a civic square in the centre of town means that there is no suitable outdoor venue for public performances or markets.
(Photo by courtesy of John Glenn Photography.)

Below: As the extract from an 1863 Ordnance Survey Map shows, there was a market square until it was taken as a site for a new City Hall at the beginning of the twentieth century.
(Map reproduced by courtesy of Ordnance Survey.)

As these three artist's impressions show, the removal of a large part of the City Hall, after the construction of a new Concert Hall at Horse Cross, would create an opportunity for an attractive and useful civic space at the heart of the city centre.
    (Courtesy of Richard Rees Building Design Partnership)

Bibliography

Campbell, D.G.: *Thomas Hay Marshall and The Making of Georgian Perth,*
    AK Bell Library 1985.

Charles, Prince of Wales: *A Vision of Britain,* 1989.

Cowan, C.: *The Ancient Capital of Scotland,* 1904.

Fothergill, R.: *The Inches of Perth.*

Girouard, M.: *Big Jim. The Life and Work of James Stirling,* 1998.

Lynch M. and Spearman, M. eds.: *The Scottish Medieval Town,* 1988.

MacDonald, A.R.: 'The Valuable Branch of the Common Good: The Forestry
    Plantation of Eighteenth Century Perth'
    (*Scottish Forrestry* Vol 51, No 1 Spring 1997).

Marshall, W.: *Historic Scenes in Perthshire,* 1881.

Pupils of Caledonian Road School: *What's in a Name? A Survey of Perth Street
    Names,* 1979.

Scruton, R: *The Classical Vernacular. Architectural Principles in an Age of
    Nihilism,* 1994.

Smith, D. Crawford: *The Historians of Perth,* 1906.

Smout, T.C.: *A History of the Scottish People 1560–1830,* 1969.

Stavert, M.: *Perth—A Short History,* Perth and Kinross District Libraries, 1991.

Urquhart, A.R. ed.: *Auld Perth,* 1906.

Vasey, P.G.: 'The Economy and Social Geography of Perth in the late
    Seventeenth and early Eighteenth centuries' (A thesis submitted for the
    University of Stirling, 1987).

Walker, D.: 'Lost Splendours of the Fair City'
    (Article in *Country Life* 3 October 1968).